T0088768

ALSO BY MARK SPECTOR

The Battle of Alberta: The Historic Rivalry Between the Edmonton Oilers and the Calgary Flames

ROAD TO GOLD

The Untold Story of Canada at the World Juniors

MARK SPECTOR

Published by Simon & Schuster
New York London Toronto Sydney New Delhi

Simon & Schuster Canada
A Division of Simon & Schuster, Inc.
166 King Street East, Suite 300
Toronto, Ontario M5A 1J3

This Simon & Schuster Canada edition November 2020

SIMON & SCHUSTER CANADA and colophon are trademarks of Simon & Schuster, Inc.

For information about special discounts for bulk purchases, please contact Simon & Schuster Special Sales at 1-800-268-3216 or CustomerService@simonandschuster.ca.

Manufactured in the United States of America

10 9 8 7 6 5 4 3 2 1

Library and Archives Canada Cataloguing in Publication
Title: Road to gold : the untold story of Canada at the World Juniors / Mark Spector.
Names: Spector, Mark, 1965– author.
Description: Simon & Schuster Canada edition. | Originally published: 2019.
Identifiers: Canadiana 2020020176X | ISBN 9781982111526 (softcover)
Subjects: LCSH: World Junior Championships (Hockey)—History. | LCSH: Hockey—Tournaments—History. |
LCSH: Hockey—Canada—History.
Classification: DDC 796.962/62—dc23

ISBN 978-1-9821-1151-9
ISBN 978-1-9821-1152-6 (pbk)
ISBN 978-1-9821-1153-3 (ebook)

To my dear wife, Shelka, who supports me through these book-writing months with love, patience, and pierogies.

To our children, Haley, Jayce, Landon, and Rudy, who have grown into successful, unique adults. And a Goldie named Wrigley, who always wandered into my office just when I needed a break.

And to so many friends across the hockey world who provided a number, a memory, a column, or a quote. There may be just one name on the jacket, but there are hundreds in my heart.

Thank you all.

CONTENTS

ROAD
TO
GOLD

CHAPTER 1

The Meeting

"If you do this right, we'll have success.
And with your good players, we will have success."

—MURRAY COSTELLO

Murray Costello sat in a chair off the lobby of Ottawa's old Skyline Hotel, watching the junior hockey owners and executives file past. They walked by on their way to the meeting room, and he smiled. They emerged for a bathroom break, and he nodded. He was clearly available for a chat. But they wouldn't break stride.

Nine o'clock became ten o'clock with no change. Costello had a copy of *The Globe and Mail* open in front of him, but he barely registered the articles, instead staring over the top of the paper as he staked out the lobby, like a secret agent in an old *Get Smart* episode. His focus was on the double doors of the meeting room across the hall, waiting for his moment.

The problem was, that moment wasn't preordained. Inside the meeting room, the owners and operators of Canada's Major Junior Hockey teams were gathered for their annual general meeting. Most of them had arrived in Ottawa completely oblivious to Costello and the pitch that he and his lieutenant, Dennis McDonald, had formulated over at the Canadian Amateur Hockey Association. The owners had their own issues, generally of the micro variety, and they weren't exactly falling over themselves to include Costello in their day.

"I sat there for a long time," Costello said. "I wondered at times, 'What the hell am I doing?' "

What the hell *was* Costello doing there? To some degree, even he wasn't sure.

It was May 1981. The New York Islanders and Edmonton Eskimos ruled their respective leagues. The PC, or personal computer, would be introduced to the world later that year. The movie *Raiders of the Lost Ark* was about to dominate the box office. The virus that causes AIDS was identified. Frequent flyer miles were invented.

And the World Junior Hockey Championships, as Canadians know them today, were born.

The tournament had been around since 1973, though it was no more popular among Canadian hockey fans than were the Izvestia Cup and the Swedish Games. In those early days, there was no guarantee the CBC would even televise the games. If Canada was in the gold medal game, it might be on TV. If not, then CBC Radio would broadcast the game. Maybe.

It didn't help that Canada was rarely in the gold medal game, so most coverage of the tournament was purely academic. No one wanted to see the Soviets play Czechoslovakia back in 1981. Even the ratings for Canadian games were sketchy.

That indifference was killing Costello, a bespectacled, greying lifetime hockey man who was not quite fifty back in 1981. Costello was sick and tired of watching the antiquated Canadian national program produce ill-prepared teams that couldn't compete with Russia, the reigning hockey superpower, at the World Juniors. He knew that Canada could—should—be the best hockey nation in the world.

Costello was the president of the Canadian Amateur Hockey Association, the forerunner to what is today called Hockey Canada. The CAHA was responsible for growing hockey in Canada, through both its programs that certified coaches from coast to coast and its organized age-group hockey from which the best kids would graduate to the junior ranks.

Each year, the CAHA and its thousands of volunteers tilled the fields, planted the seeds, and tended the crops of the hockey world's most fecund soil—Canada—and then, when the best of the harvest reached Major Junior Hockey, the junior operators would pat the CAHA on the head and say, "We'll take it from here."

Costello and McDonald, his right-hand man at the CAHA, had watched this happen year after year. And for every bit as long, they watched as the Canadian junior team was doomed to failure.

Since the World Juniors tournament's inception in 1974, when the International Ice Hockey Federation invited five nations to join Russia's Under-20 team in what was then known as Leningrad (today it is Saint Petersburg), Canada had obliged by sending over its reigning Memorial Cup champions, plus a few last-minute pick-ups, to the tournament. There, Canada's best junior team from the previous season would promptly get toasted.

The problems were many, and they were systemic.

The team that won the Memorial Cup in May tended to lose its best nineteen-year-old players the following season, when they turned pro. Sometimes, even the best eighteen-year-olds from the team would head to the National Hockey League, leaving that year's champion without its best players at the World Juniors tournament in December.

There was also the culture shock. In the early days of the tournament, none of the kids had played on the larger European ice surface, and few of their coaches had any experience with game-planning for the different style of hockey played by the Europeans.

Even more foreign than the host country's culture, though, was the on-ice officiating.

"Teams going over had no idea what they were going to face," Costello said. "If you hit a guy hard, even if it was clean, it would be a penalty simply because it was a hard hit. And the European teams used the basketball pick play, where a guy would come in and block someone out. Over here, that would be an interference penalty, but they wouldn't call it over there. Our players got frustrated, and of course the sticks would get going, and we'd then pay the price on the special teams."

By the time the Canadian boys figured out what constituted a penalty, the team was often out of contention for the gold. And even in years like 1977 and '78, when Canada medaled, there was still one final, intractable problem: We couldn't beat the Russians.

As the head of the CAHA, Costello was the liaison between the International Ice Hockey Federation (IIHF) and the Canadian junior leagues. From his vantage point, he could clearly see the inherent negatives that accompanied sending over what was effectively just an enhanced club team, as opposed to a true national team. The rotating coaching staffs were fresh each year, which meant they encountered every problem for the first time, learned the hard lesson, and then were replaced by another bunch of first-timers the next year. Then those coaches would relearn the same lessons. There was no one to collect the intel and pass it down. No mechanism for amassing accrued knowledge.

Costello likened the process to soccer, where players earned a "cap" for every international game they played. "We were playing every year with zero caps," he said. "We had to break this cycle, to prepare our players and coaches to be able to play the international game."

For Costello, the final straw had come a few months before the Skyline Hotel meeting, as he watched the 1981 tournament unfold in what was then West Germany. The reigning Memorial Cup winners, the Cornwall Royals—a team that included Dale Hawerchuk, Doug Gilmour, and a nineteen-year-old Marc Crawford—added a few players from the Quebec Major Junior Hockey League (QMJHL) and boarded a flight for Fussen, Germany. There, they played the best Under-20 national teams from seven other countries. When the dust settled, Canada finished in seventh place—ahead of only Austria.

"When Germany beat Canada [7–6 in the Consolation Round], with Dale Hawerchuk on the team, I thought, 'That's just not fair to him, and it's not fair to Canada,'" Costello said. "I said to myself, 'We *have* to do something.'"

Costello had seen this moment coming for a few years, but losing to West Germany and finishing seventh shed a particularly bad light on the CAHA. Seriously? This was Canada. We could handle seventh place on the ski hill, or the soccer pitch. But this was hockey, the one sport where we can say—and truly believe—that we are better than any other nation on earth.

"The only thing we could do was to leave the club team system,"

Costello said. "We were sending former winners over to represent Canada, and more and more they were starting to get embarrassed by their performance over there. We had to get some form of either a regional or national team."

So, Costello had come to the Skyline on a reclamation mission. He wanted some players back. Not many players, and not for very long. Just an All-Star team of the very best junior players, who would be made available over the Christmas holidays. He didn't need junior hockey to totally grind to a halt during the international tournament. The leagues could continue without their best players, whom Costello would take overseas.

That was the plan, at least. But to make it a reality, Costello first had to get through those double doors and into the meeting room, where the real test lay.

Behind those closed doors sat the heads of the three junior leagues: David Branch of the Ontario Hockey League; Ed Chynoweth from the Western Hockey League; and Jean Rougeau of the Quebec Major Junior Hockey League. The three junior execs had watched the years of failed World Juniors experiences unfold from a position of passive interest. Sure, each year, one of their teams was involved in the tournament. But they were each running a business whose profits were largely gate-driven in junior markets across Canada and the U.S. What was happening at Christmas in faraway places was of a modicum of concern, but not much more.

"They didn't want to let me into the meeting," Costello said. "I thought, 'I'm going to wait and see if you will.'"

So Costello sat out in the hallway as hockey man after hockey man marched past dismissively. The clock ticked. The owners left for and returned from lunch. Still, Costello didn't budge. He'd worked too long at this to simply go away.

In the previous months, Costello had put in time forging relationships with the three junior league commissioners. When they were together as a larger group, they were a united front against the idea of a national team—they rallied around their concerns about the possibility of star junior players getting injured, and their reluctance to lose talent during the lucrative Christmas schedule always won the day. Costello felt that each exec would be more open to his concepts if he approached them individually. Long before he had arrived at the Skyline, Costello had been pleased to discover that their tune changed in a one-on-one setting. That the idea of revamping the World Juniors system actually intrigued them.

In his work behind the scenes, though, Costello had also discovered that each of the leagues was largely a shoestring operation. Costello was an expert at this, as the CAHA was perennially broke as well. He knew that he'd have enough trouble securing support from the junior operators if he were flush, but broke there was no chance. So, weeks before he pitched the junior operators at the Skyline, Costello had gone down the street to the office of Sport Canada, where he met a man named Peter Lesaux.

"We're not giving any money to you guys," Lesaux told Costello. "You just deal in recreational hockey. Friendly hockey. The national government shouldn't be supporting that kind of programming."

"Peter," Costello asked, "how is it that the ski teams and the swim teams have training camps in South America in the off-season to prepare for competition?"

"That's because they have programs that are leading to the Olympics, where they have a reasonable chance of getting medals. That's what we fund," Lesaux said.

Costello dug in. "So if we can give you a program where we would be more successful and more prominent in international competition, would you be prepared to fund that?"

Lesaux pondered the idea. "We'd give you seed money. Not something you could count on every year, but seed money."

Costello had what he needed. "Can we have another meeting in a week?" he asked, before leaving.

In that week, Costello and McDonald brought together years of loose thoughts, planning, and dreams, cementing it all into a plan. They produced clear plastic sheets—transparencies, as they were called back in the day—to help with their presentation. The first sheet showed how they would build the footings for national teams at the Under-18, Under-20, and Olympic level hockey in Year 1, and the next sheet went over top with the plans for Year 2, then Year 3, and so on. It led all the way to success at the Olympic level.

When Costello and McDonald returned the next week, Lesaux wasn't the only one in the room. Several of his Sport Canada colleagues joined the meeting, no doubt intrigued by their organization's budding partnership with the national body that represented Canada's largest participatory sport—and of course, its national game.

Costello and McDonald laid out their dream, plastic sheet overtop of plastic sheet. Lesaux was impressed.

"Yes," Lesaux said when the pair was finished. "We would fund something like that. We can give you a couple of hundred grand. But don't count on it every year."

"Don't worry," Costello said. "You give us a shot at this, we'll get it going, and we won't have to come back to you."

Now the CAHA had some money. But it wouldn't be much use if they could not access the best junior-aged players in Canada.

The plan was simple, and similar to what Hockey Canada employs today: hold a summer camp with forty or so of the best junior players, scout them through the first one-third of their season, and bring twenty-seven or twenty-eight of them back for a pre-Christmas camp. Team Canada would make some final cuts and leave around December 20 for Europe, or wherever the tournament was being held.

That massive change in protocol would require an equally huge leap of faith by the junior governors, but as the hours ticked by inside the Skyline, Costello couldn't even get inside the door to speak with them. Had this been the first time he'd met these men, Costello might have rotted in that chair out in the hallway. But he'd been preparing for that one meeting for a year, and he had an inkling that, even if the junior operators weren't letting on that they kind of liked this Costello guy, in their own heads they were all looking to give him a fair shake.

"I'd talked to each of them, separately, before that, three or four times each," Costello said. "Mainly Ed. He would take my call and always kept the door open, whereas the others would kind of go silent on you. With Ed, I could keep the dialogue going. He became a key guy."

Ed Chynoweth, who died in 1988, ran the WHL out of Calgary. He was a big, imposing man—six-foot-two with a boiler to match—and an intimidating presence. Big Ed told you what he thought in plain, Western Canadian English. He was the last guy some bureaucrat from Ottawa was going to dictate anything to.

"He was quick with a quip, and always had a smart-ass answer to give back to you," Costello recalled. "At first we butted heads. It didn't seem like we would ever find common ground."

Costello, fortunately, was a deal maker. Dumb like a fox, he knew when to comply, when to give something back to build the relationship, and when to apply some pressure with whatever means he had available.

So, in his early one-on-ones with Chynoweth, Costello steered the conversation towards Ed's son, Dean, who was only thirteen years old, still five or six years away from a trip to the World Juniors.

"I knew, talking to Ed, about the effect a true national team would have on parents. He had to have some feeling for that. So I told him, 'Wouldn't it be a great opportunity for Dean to get a chance to represent his country internationally and then come back and play for his junior team? He'd be a bigger player for his team with that experience.' How can you go against that?"

Ed didn't give in, and he would not promise Costello a place on the agenda of the meetings scheduled for the Skyline. But when Big Ed gave him the date, time, and location—in case Costello were to make a surprise appearance—Costello knew he'd made a sizeable dent in the façade.

With that new information in hand, Costello trained his gaze on Rougeau, who served as the QMJHL's president. Rougeau had just begun his tenure as the head of the Q, the top junior league in Quebec, but he was already making a name for himself. To this day, the Jean Rougeau Trophy is the Q's version of the President's Trophy, given to the team that finishes with the most points each season.

By far the most interesting section of Rougeau's resume, however, was his time as a member of Quebec's legendary wrestling family. He wrestled professionally under the name "Johnny" Rougeau, and his two nephews, Jacques and Raymond, would find fame in the World Wrestling Federation as the "Fabulous Rougeau Brothers."

"We're not trying to do anything to hurt Major Junior Hockey," Costello explained to Rougeau. "In fact, we really think that if you go along with this, we can build Major Junior Hockey. We can help you."

"I like what you're saying, giving kids an opportunity to play for their country," Rougeau told Costello. "But I'm not sure I'll be able to sell anyone else on this." He paused. "If you get the meeting you're looking for, I may ask you some questions to keep the conversation going. Understand: I'm not against you, even though it may sound like I am."

Check! Costello had Rougeau, to some extent, in his corner.

That left only Branch, the youngest of the three junior leaders. Just thirty-three years old, Branch was not so entrenched in tradition. Costello suspected that, as a relative newcomer, Branch would likely follow whatever course was set by Chynoweth.

So Costello had some Sport Canada money, and some currency with the people he would need to convince of his plan. Yet here he was, halfway through the afternoon, still sitting out in the hallway of the Skyline, like Gretzky on the bench in the 1998 Olympic shoot-out. As the enigmatic Petr Klíma once said, "You need a long stick to score from the press box." How true: Costello wasn't converting anyone from out in the foyer.

"I had to give these guys my best shot," Costello said. "To know that we at least tried the best we could. There was no alternative. We were going to have to get those players one way or another."

As the day went on, the hockey men trickled out of the meeting room. Eventually, all of the team owners were gone, but the three principals remained: Chynoweth, Rougeau, and Branch.

"To be honest, I think Ed became a bit embarrassed that I was sitting there all that time and not even getting a nod, or some recognition from anyone," Costello said. "Finally, they let me into the meeting. It was at least two-thirty, maybe after three, when they let me in."

Finally! Costello walked through the double doors and stepped into the room to present. His initial impression was less than promising.

"It wasn't that they weren't happy that I was there," Costello recalled. "They were just paying me a courtesy to allow me to have a shot. They were going to hear what I had to say, then shut down the meeting and go home."

Costello realized that this was likely going to be the only shot he would get. He had nothing to lose.

"Look, guys," Costello began. "This isn't anything that would work against you guys. This can make you look good. If you do this right, we'll have success. And with your good players, we *will* have success."

To Costello's credit, history records him as an oracle. The picture he painted for the CHL execs hangs figuratively in every Major Junior rink in Canada and the United States today. In fact, it is a brighter, more lucrative picture even than Costello imagined.

"You'll have guys coming home after Christmas with a gold medal around their necks, probably the captain of their teams," Costello told the three junior league execs. "The first game they play when they come back, you could have them go out in the warm-up with the national team jersey on, not the club team. He'll have a gold medal around his neck, and you can introduce him to the crowd. Have the mayor do the face-off, recognizing the accomplishment of this young lad in his community. This will do nothing but sell your game. Your brand would be broadcast further than ever before as the best junior league in the world!"

Costello could sense some traction. It seemed that some of the seeds he had sown were beginning to germinate. Rougeau, the old wrestler, was adept at playing the heel, and he came off the top rope at Costello.

"Who the hell are you to be doing this? This is our area!" Rougeau snarled at Costello.

Costello knew that Rougeau's bark was worse than his bite. Just as Rougeau had promised, he was asking questions to keep the conversation going.

It worked. Ed jumped in immediately after. "You don't know what you're doing!" he told Costello. "You work for a bunch of volunteers! Most of them don't know what they're doing. Why should we be working with you guys?"

"Those volunteers keep it going every Saturday, Sunday at six, seven o'clock in the morning," Costello responded. "If they didn't do that, the kids would have no interest in the game, and you owners would have no future. You owe something to the players, to give them the best opportunity to be what they can become. Why don't you look at it that way?"

The owners didn't let up. They were in the business of making money, and in their minds, Costello and the rest of the Canadian Amateur Hockey Association were in the business of development. They couldn't see a way to make a profit from that, so back and forth they went, as Costello tried not to lose his cool.

"If we didn't develop kids, you wouldn't have any leagues," Costello said. "You've got to have some appreciation for what we do. Every company invests something in research and development. Don't you guys have to do some of that, too?"

It was difficult for any of the junior men to find holes in Costello's arguments thus far, even if they were reluctant to let on. Costello sensed as much, so he pushed forward, proving not only that the CAHA—really, he and McDonald—had put a lot of preparatory thought into this, but that they could further be trusted to competently run the program, should the CHL agree to go ahead.

The CAHA was steeped in experience of arranging high-level tournaments across Canada. They knew exactly what could be improved when it came to sending a team into competition at the WJHC. In the past, coaches had shouldered the role of team managers, arranging buses, meals, practice times, and all of the other day-to-day logistics for the team. Such skills weren't usually a coach's strength, and worse, they diverted their attention from their coaching duties.

Costello laid out a new idea for managing the team, one that Dennis had come up with. "If we're going to get the best coach we can get, we should remove all those responsibilities and bring him there only to coach, because that's the talent we want from him. We'll put the rest of the people in place to handle all of the logistics, to the *n*th detail. All the coach will have to do is coach."

Costello could almost see the thought bubbles forming above the heads of his audience. Then, they asked—no, they demanded—that if the program went forward, the junior leagues would get to appoint the general manager of the team. After all, that was how junior franchises were run. The National Junior Team wasn't one of their franchises, however, and Costello and McDonald had it planned out a different way.

"If you put a manager in there, he's going to make some decisions that the coach will use as an excuse," Costello said. "When we get a coach in there, we've got to hold his feet to the fire. Anyone can pick the first twelve players for the National Junior Team. But what makes a gold medal team is the last eight. Those last eight have to be the choices of the coaching staff. If the coaching staff goes to war with the guys they chose, they won't have an excuse."

It seemed that the CAHA had thought of everything. Costello made a mental note to thank McDonald again when he got back to the office.

"Dennis McDonald never got the credit that he should have gotten for a lot of the details behind the scenes," Costello said. "He was instrumental in the whole thing."

By now, dinner hour was closing in, and like any coach, Costello knew when he was losing his audience. The junior league presidents had heard him out, but they weren't exactly gushing at the thought of joining forces with the CAHA or putting their best players at risk of injury in a bunch of games that no Canadian was even watching. And before they left, there was one more problem to discuss: the timing.

"You play a lot of games over the Christmas holidays, because there's no school," Branch said. "People are looking for things to do, and clearly in all our markets, it's a huge time."

Costello had spent most of his bullets. So, in a last ditch effort, he brought out the heavy artillery.

"You guys are really playing a tough game here," Costello said. "If you say absolutely no, that you're not going to do it, I'm going to start talking to the parents of those kids. If I tell a parent that their son has a chance to wear the national team jersey and represent his country, but his team will not let him go, you guys are going to be in trouble."

An empty threat? No sir, it was not. Costello had tried out that exact angle once before, on a trip to Red Deer, Alberta.

"A guy by the name of John Moller had two sons playing junior: Randy and Mike. Both good players," Costello recalled. "I said to John, 'I'd really like to see your sons have a chance to play for their country, but the WHL is telling us that they can't do it.' John said to me: 'Nobody is going to tell my sons they can't play for their country.'"

Back at the Skyline, Costello continued to outline the journey that he and McDonald had mapped out. It included a committee that would oversee the national program. At the mention of that, the junior leagues sensed an opening to gain a bit of power over the CAHA.

"If we do give you a shot at this, to see if it might work, we want to be an integral part of the National Junior Team Policy Committee," Branch said. "We'd put forward one person from each league for the board."

With three of the four spots on the committee going to the junior hockey execs and the CAHA holding the fourth, Costello knew he was putting himself in a position of weakness. But the three junior league presidents promised him that they would be fair. So he acquiesced, but with one caveat.

"I'll go along with this and make you guys members of the National Team Policy Committee, and I'll chair it," Costello told the men. "But if you guys do anything to undermine the program that we're trying to get going, I'll pull the money. Because the money comes from the government to us, not to you. The thing will go down the drain, and you guys will wear it if it happens that way."

The league commissioners agreed. It had been one hell of a negotiation, but somehow, Costello had emerged not only with his plan intact, but with a reasonable amount of control over the newborn Program of Excellence. He'd arrived at the Skyline that day just hoping to get inside that boardroom, and when he walked out in the Ottawa night, he had to admit: This felt very much like success.

Or, at least, tempered success. Costello had convinced the heads of the three junior leagues to look into the future of Canadian junior hockey and play ball, but the individual owners would prove to be another story.

"There was still lot of animosity toward this happening," Costello said. "A lot of junior owners, they didn't want any part of this. 'They're our players and they're under contract to us. They can't be going to play for anyone else.'"

The stress of getting inside that meeting to talk the talk now paled in comparison to the pressure that Costello and McDonald felt to make their new Program of Excellence walk the walk.

"We still realized it was a tentative thing," McDonald said. "We now had to make it work."

CHAPTER 2

A Glimpse of Success

"It was an awful rendition of the anthem.
One of the best ones I've ever been a part of."

—MIKE MOLLER

With the Skyline meeting in the rearview mirror and the blueprint in place, the Program of Excellence was still a long way from living up to its name. It had uncertain, temporary funding, a group of junior owners who were less than convinced, and a model that had never before been attempted in Canada. Like the Blues Brothers, McDonald and Costello were on a mission from God.

Luckily, McDonald already had the course mapped out. He and Costello made Dave Draper their head scout. Draper was tasked with going countrywide during the season to rate the junior players, one to fifty, for summer camp invites. A summer camp would be held at Queen's University in Kingston, Ontario, and the final twenty-three-man group would then be invited to Winnipeg for a mid-December camp.

The next bone of contention became the coaches. The CHL wouldn't part with any of its coaches for the World Juniors team—the first sign of a tepid buy-in by the junior operators, who weren't bending over backward to staff this maiden voyage. So, Costello reached out to Dave King at the University of Saskatchewan, who accepted the job. His assistants were Mike Keenan, then serving with the Rochester Americans of the AHL, and Jacques Lemaire, the recent Montreal Canadiens great who was beginning a second career as a coach. New jobs and other commitments meant that neither assistant would be with the team come Christmas, but their being at that initial camp lent much-needed chops to what King was trying to build.

"Mike and Jacques gave us real good credibility. Some names to attach to the concept," King said. "It was all part of the sell. We were trying to sell this concept to the Major Junior clubs and to the public, and it wasn't going to be easy."

Costello and McDonald had given Dave King the keys to the car. The ignition, alternator, transmission, and gas, though—all of that was supposed to come later. Or so King hoped.

Much as Costello had sold the Major Junior operators the dream of a national junior team on concepts and suppositions, the first U-20 head coach in the history of the Program of Excellence was tasked with holding the inaugural summer camp amid an environment of uncertainty and quasi-mistrust.

In August of 1981, forty-four players arrived at Queen's University for a summer camp that Costello and McDonald knew would be the first essential building block in differentiating the 1982 World Juniors team from all the Memorial Cup champs who had tried and failed to win an IIHF Under-20 tournament since 1974.

Costello knew that they would need every single one of Canada's elite U-20 players to get their Frankenstein up off the table. But that was easier said than done.

For instance, King wanted a nineteen-year-old out of Viking, Alberta, named Brent Sutter to be on the team. But Sutter was a first-round pick of the Islanders in 1980 and had been promised by Islanders GM Bill Torrey that there was a post-Christmas call-up in the offing if he stayed with the Lethbridge Broncos and eschewed the World Juniors camp. The respectful Sutter—who would pile up 80 points in just thirty-four WHL games that season before receiving the promised call-up—heeded Mr. Torrey's advice and stayed home. Ironically, Sutter would eventually get his fill of World Juniors experience, named as head coach for three editions of Team Canada, in 2005, 2006, and 2014.

Another player who didn't see the value in attending was Edmonton-born Ken Yaremchuk, who would go on to a 157-point season with the Portland Winterhawks that year. Yaremchuk was the kind of player who would be all over Team Canada in its modern guise, but he wasn't jumping at the opportunity back in 1981. It evidences how the tournament just didn't have the cultural traction it does today—not in Canadian society, not even in hockey society. None of the kids being asked to try out for the team had grown up gathering around the television every Christmas to watch the World Juniors, the way a Jordan Eberle or Connor McDavid would years later.

"The Major Junior teams were still really concerned about this concept. And they had some very legitimate concerns," said the ever-polite Dave King. "So at the camp in Kingston, we had a mixed bag. We had quite a few guys from U.S. colleges, because out of the Major

Junior ranks, a lot of teams were not at all willing to let their players come to the camp.

"We understood what we were getting into. We knew it wasn't going to be a big seal of approval where everyone jumped on board," he said. "We knew it was going to be a tough sell. We knew we were going to get some of the best players, but not all of them. But you've got to start the concept. Get it kicked off. That's what this was. A big 'let's go . . .'"

Costello and McDonald had, of course, been thinking several steps ahead all the while. In the spring of 1981, they'd sent King to the senior World Championships in Gothenburg, Sweden. They asked him to scout the European teams and their systems, the exact areas where a dearth of knowledge had sunk so many Canadian entries in tournaments past.

"They wanted me to get some international experience, and see some international hockey," said King, a young Clare Drake disciple who would continue to lean on the venerable University of Alberta coach for advice.

When the August camp concluded and all the players returned home to prepare for their various training camps across Canada and the U.S., the plan was for Hockey Canada to watch the forty-four summer camp participants as they embarked upon their seasons. And of course, to keep an eye out for someone who might emerge in the first couple of months, a player whom perhaps they had missed who would be helpful come Christmastime.

But there was one problem: Dave Draper was only one man, and the coaching staff all had full-time jobs and their own teams to worry about. Scouting the entire CHL, plus any Canadians playing in American college hockey, was too big a task. So the program hooked up with the National Hockey League's central scouting service—

more specifically, with Jim Gregory—to keep King informed on the eligible U-20 players while he was tied to his work coaching the University of Saskatchewan Huskies.

"In those days you just couldn't download games and watch them," King said. "So, Jim Gregory was really important in helping us to further identify our list."

Today Hockey Canada has a head scout, regional scouts, and the wherewithal to keep track of every eligible Canadian player who has even the slightest possibility of making Team Canada. But in December 1981, the relative uncertainty that had prevailed in Kingston was still in the air when King and his staff opened the first-ever edition of a Program of Excellence December selection camp, at the old Max Bell Arena—the Winnipeg home of the University of Manitoba Bisons.

Among the roughly thirty players who checked into camp, there were varying degrees of knowledge about what they were getting themselves into.

"The World Juniors didn't mean anything to me at that time," said Troy Murray, who was playing for the University of North Dakota Fighting Sioux in 1982. "We just didn't know anything about it. I don't think it was a very significant tournament in anyone's mind, back in those days. For us it was foreign. For the coaches, too. Everything was new.

"Even when the tournament started we really didn't know what to expect. For all the players on the team, there was no protocol prior to 1982."

Well, maybe not for everybody. Mike Moller and his brother, Randy—the sons of John Moller, whom Costello had invoked in his pitch at the Skyline—were both playing junior at the time, and for them, the tournament was a unique opportunity.

"My dad, John, who passed away a few years ago, was a former RCMP," Mike said. "Being a former policeman, he knew what it was about to serve your community. Or your town. Or your country. He said, 'You've never had the chance to play for your country before. You've never had the opportunity to put the jersey on.' "

There was no question in the Moller household whether sons Mike and Randy would leave the Lethbridge Broncos during the Christmas season. Broncos head coach John Chapman would have to make do without two of his best players.

"What were these junior teams going to do? Suspend all of us? Me and my brother, Randy, we were going to go," Mike said. "Everybody thought they knew what was the right thing to do at the time. But don't you think that having a young player playing a World Championship would not only help him as a player, but maybe it would come back to your team and help here, too? And the profile of your team? Can you not use that publicity?"

Not everyone shared the Mollers' outlook, though, and the team had some work to do if the kind of ceremony Costello had predicted—junior players returning after New Year's and the mayor dropping the ceremonial puck—was ever going to take place. So they rolled up their sleeves and got after it that December in Winnipeg.

Sensing that the program was gaining some traction, the junior leagues took on a little bit more ownership at the December camp, dispatching Sherry Bassin, the GM of the Oshawa Generals from the OHL, and Georges Larivière, from the Quebec Ice Hockey Federation, to oversee the camp. It was a weird time: The CAHA had begun to build the framework of something special by bringing all the best junior players together, but outside the walls of the Program of Excellence, few Canadians had a clue what was brewing.

If the sizzle was questionable, however, the steak was highly legit.

The level of player fixing to wear those Team Canada uniforms was undeniably top notch.

"Al MacInnis was my roommate there," Troy Murray said. "Gerard Gallant was there, and Tony Tanti. I was going, 'Wow, I'm in way over my head here.'"

Tanti would get injured and did not stick with the team. As for Gallant and MacInnis? "It's the old expression," King said. "We went in another direction."

To cut MacInnis was the tougher decision of the two, King recalled, but at the time, his blue-line had a lot of mobility. It being 1981, the coaching staff felt a need for a stay-at-home, physical guy. Garth Butcher got the job, and MacInnis took his legendary blast back to the Kitchener Rangers, where he bombed in 25 goals in just fifty-nine games, while adding 50 assists. That season, he would join the Calgary Flames for the first two games of what would become a distinguished 1,416-game NHL career.

"They're hard choices," King admitted. "But I've got to tell you, look at Butcher's penalty minutes in the NHL [2,302 in 897 NHL games]. He had four penalty minutes in that tournament, as I recall. [The statistics show Butcher as having zero PIMs in the 1982 tournament.] He played really disciplined and made a real difference. I guess the end result justifies the means."

As camp broke, and the cuts were made, King poked the bear one more time when he decided on Troy Murray as his captain. If there's still an element of politics today surrounding the selection of NCAA players to Team Canada (and there is) because they have eschewed the CHL as their chosen route to the NHL, well, in 1981, choosing a college kid to be the first captain under the new Program of Excellence was sheer heresy.

"Troy was just automatically a leader, and through the course of our camp it became clear he would be our captain," King said matter-of-factly. "It didn't matter where he played. We never discussed that. We said, 'He's the best guy.'"

"Dave King called me in and said I was going to be captain," Murray recalled. "I was completely blown away. It was something I did not expect, whatsoever."

Neither did Western League boss Ed Chynoweth and his junior colleagues.

"I know it was not a hugely popular decision," Murray admitted. "But [the coaching staff] said, 'No, this is our captain. This is who we feel is the best player to lead this team.' They backed it up—backed me up—against some big junior names."

So, with the leadership group in place and Christmas Day around the corner, it was time for the Program of Excellence to show people what it had. How it was truly going to be a better system, as Costello had promised. How it was going to set things straight for Canada at the U-20 level and put the country back at the centre of the international hockey map.

The World Juniors that year were based in nearby Minnesota. But just as the 1975 tournament was shared by Winnipeg, Brandon, Minneapolis, Bloomington, and Fargo, North Dakota, the 1982 tournament was played in arenas scattered across Minnesota and Manitoba, with a couple of games played across state and provincial lines. Team Canada would play its first three games at the old Winnipeg Arena, just another small bit of fortune that graced the birthing of the CAHA's new baby.

It meant that the initial foray for the Program of Excellence into the international hockey marketplace would take place on Canadian-sized ice surfaces. As such, the ol' 200 x 85 made this a rare World Juniors where the Euros would have to learn to adapt to the North American sheet, rather than the usual process of Canadian players figuring out the nuances of the 200 x 100-foot ice.

"First off," said King, "to play our first three games at the Winnipeg Arena, those are home games for us. And then the small rink—at least there was no adaptation to that. We were comfortable in the confines of the smaller ice surface. It was a real help to our team for sure."

Winnipeg was an accomplished host of international hockey, having accommodated Game 3 of the 1972 Summit Series. That night, under the gaze of that giant portrait of Queen Elizabeth, which hung from the rafters in all of its 5-by-7 metres of glory, Team Canada had blown leads of 3–1 and 4–2 before settling for a 4–4 tie.

Further cementing Winnipeg as Canada's forerunner in international hockey relations was the fact the Winnipeg Jets had been the most forward-thinking team in the World Hockey Association. The city had put together a European-laden lineup that included the likes of Ulf and Kent Nilsson, Anders Hedberg, Lars-Erik Sjöberg, and Willy Lindström.

Those Jets dominated the old WHA, winning three of the last four Avco Cups as league champions, and history records that Glen Sather—whose Edmonton Oilers lost the final Avco Cup to Winnipeg—patterned his NHL Oilers after the free-flow, European style of play that had worked so well in Manitoba.

In 1982, the home-ice advantage was a welcome opportunity for the World Juniors team to get their sea legs under them. Because they had finished in seventh place the year before in Fussen, Germany (a city that has never been kind to Canada's World Juniors fortunes),

Canada was forced to play its toughest opponents right at the start of the 1982 tournament.

Back then, the tournament began before Christmas, a departure from the traditional Boxing Day start we have come to know today. Canada opened on December 22 with a 5–1 win over Team Finland, which was led by future NHLers Raimo Summanen and Petri Skriko.

"From Day 1 to when we got to the tournament, it had really picked up steam," Troy Murray remembered. "When the tournament started, we had packed houses. . . . The tournament started to build and build. You started to get some notoriety across Canada, with different media [outlets] coming in, because you had players from across Canada. The atmosphere in Winnipeg was just amazing. It was sold out. The place was packed."

Next up was Sweden. The Swedes had plenty of talent, including future Montreal Canadien Kjell Dahlin and soon-to-be Philadelphia Flyer Pelle Eklund. The Canadian team wasn't prepared for the threat they'd pose. There was no internet to gather intel or watch video, and European juniors didn't regularly come over to play in the CHL or the NCAA, as they do today—in fact, most of the European teams didn't even have name bars on their jerseys.

"I couldn't name one player on any of the other teams," Murray said. "Honestly. It was something that I never even thought about. I was playing college, and these guys weren't ever going to play in the NHL, right? They weren't your competition."

On December 23 in Winnipeg, however, the Swedes were plenty of competition. As it turned out, they were a much tougher foe than the Suomis.

"It was my first time—and likely it was the same for the majority of us players—to play a team that had that 'puck possession' style," Murray said. "I remember that they had the puck, and we couldn't get it back from them. We had to figure out how to go get it. I remember, we got frustrated because we were just chasing the play.

"But Dave King, he knew this was coming. He had the international experience. That was a game we really had to battle through to win it."

So, what were the pearls of wisdom that King concocted to get his team going? He simply did what any good Canadian coach would have done in those days, faced with an opposition roster full of fast-skating Swedes:

Canada put the body on them.

"We dialed our game up physically," King said. "Troy Murray, Garth Butcher, Gary Nylund, Gordie Kluzak—they laid some crushing body checks. Clean ones, but crushing. I want to tell you right off the top here—we were the least penalized team in that tournament. Our open-ice body checks were unbelievable, and suddenly in the last half of the game we just became more comfortable. We started to have the puck and play better. It was our physical game that really picked us up."

Canada prevailed in that game by a 3–2 score. That set up a Boxing Day tilt against the mighty Soviet Union, which had been upset by the Czechoslovaks in their second game. A Canadian win would leave them with a record of 3-0 and the Soviets at 1-2, far back in Canada's rearview mirror.

Recalled Murray: "Kinger had said, 'How we do in the first three games will dictate how we're going to do.' Well, truer words were never spoken."

The Russians were better than their record suggested, and they had won seven of the eight World Juniors that had been contested to that point. That included three "unofficial" U-20s from 1974 to 1976, then four straight "official" International Ice Hockey

Federation–sanctioned tournaments, from 1977 to 1980, before Sweden's gold medal in Fussen in 1981.

This was still the old CCCP Russians, the robotic, weaving-up-the-ice, Jofa helmet–wearing Soviets who would not place a player into the National Hockey League for nearly a decade.

"It went back to '72," said Murray, who could recall the teacher wheeling a television on a stand into his fifth-grade classroom at Sir George Simpson School in St. Albert, Alberta, to watch the final game of the Summit Series in September of 1972. "Everyone was shutting down schools in the middle of the day, bringing TVs into the classrooms, and watching that Summit Series. We all knew what the Russians were about.

"Now you look at it, and the Swedes are a world power in hockey. The Finns have had their moments [most recently a 2019 World Juniors gold in Vancouver, where they eliminated Canada in a quarter-final game]. Now, there is tradition and history within those tournaments between the Canadian teams and everyone else, because at one time or another we've had upsets and rivalries. But back then, the majority of players had never experienced international hockey before. All we knew was the Russians were the team to beat."

"At that point they still didn't have any guys playing in the NHL," Moller points out, "and all we'd heard about was how, if these guys were allowed to come over to the NHL, they'd have seven or eight guys in the NHL right now, dominating. And they had a goalie who was supposed to be so good they couldn't even score on him in practice. . . .

"Well, that really helps your confidence."

Adding to the mix of anxieties was the fact that the CBC decided to break with precedent and televise a round-robin game from the early part of the tournament. There couldn't be more pressure on the group of eighteen- and nineteen-year-olds—a refrain that would become an eternal theme of World Juniors media coverage.

Boxing Day fell on a Saturday in 1981, and the *Hockey Night in Canada* truck was set up and ready to televise a game between the Chicago Blackhawks and the Winnipeg Jets that evening. Moller, whose memory is better than most partially because of a meticulous scrapbook of the tournament kept by his parents, captured what the cameras didn't.

"The game was to be, like the first two games, only on radio. But the Blackhawks were in Winnipeg, and they were going to play the Jets on the Saturday night. Then someone had this great idea: 'Let's broadcast the Canada-Russia game at one-thirty in the afternoon!'

"I can tell you, if we had gone 0–2 and got blitzed, I don't think that game would have been shown.

"So now, not only are we playing the Russians, but everyone across Canada is going to have their TVs on. What else are they going to be doing at one-thirty on Boxing Day? Now, we don't just have to play these guys. We have to play them *in front of the whole country*.

"I was scared spitless. *Scared spitless!* That we weren't going to perform. That they were just going to be so much better, and it was going to be no contest."

"My parents flew in for that game," Murray said. "There were two Russian guys, and I just destroyed them with body checks. For whatever reason, that was the game in my mind that defined what that team was about. We played our style of game and wouldn't let them play theirs.

"We imposed our physical will. We had them backing down, and that arena was just going crazy," he said. "It went back to '72. Russia-Canada—the two hockey powers. That game had a huge buildup in Winnipeg, and we just dominated."

To hear head coach Dave King—a future NHL and KHL coach whose resume reads like a thesis paper in Canada-Russia relations—tell it, that Boxing Day game was perhaps as close to the perfect game as he's ever coached.

"I'll tell you, we just had one of those games," he said, a lifetime coach reveling in the memory of one of those days when the plan just came together perfectly. "Every player was at the top of his game. We played hard, physical, and so smart. When we made mistakes, our goaltending was right there. We got up on the Russians—suddenly it's 3–0!—and you could see that they were really confused by it. And their coaching staff was not happy. We just kept our foot on the gas. We beat 'em 7–0. It was the worst loss ever by a Russian team in international competition [Russia's worst loss to date at a U-20].

"We were almost mistake-free. It was one of those games where you say, 'Wow. Amazing.'"

Like any Canadian kid of that time, Moller had been intimidated by the prospect of meeting the Russians. But as successful athletes tend to do, he found a way to take a negative energy and make it into a positive. Moller decided that it would take the perfect game to win that day, and as the plan began to unfold seamlessly, he could feel how his teammates were being energized.

"Every stride was going to be the best stride I had. Every dump in would be perfect. We get off to a good start, we score a couple of goals, they get a little frustrated. And next thing you know, I mean, not only did we win 7–0, but by the end? They didn't even want the puck anymore."

"It probably shocked the hell out of them. It shocked us, that we could win by that kind of a score," admitted the captain, Murray. "It really galvanized our team. We'd beaten the Russians. The guys were suddenly saying, 'We might be able to do something here.'"

To that point, the WJC had been Russia's tournament. Not only had they won seven of eight tournaments, they were a true, full-time team that lived, practiced, and played together for the whole year. That this All-Star team of Canadians could not only beat them, but win in such dominant, devastating fashion did two things. In the big picture, it blew wind into the sails of the whole Program of Excellence concept. More acutely, this particular group of kids was starting to truly believe they could win this tournament.

After the win against Russia, Canada headed south of the border. That was it for Manitoba—Canada's remaining games would be played in Minnesota. And with a nice 3-0 start against the European powers, Canada found itself tied atop the standings with Czechoslovakia, two games clear of the USSR. Now, away from the din that was Winnipeg Arena, the Canadians would settle into the part of the tournament that featured fewer marquee opponents and far, far fewer fans in the seats.

The very next day in Bloomington, Canada had to come from behind to secure a 5–4 win over an American team that had all kinds of future NHLers on its roster—Chris Chelios, Phil Housley, and John Vanbiesbrouck, to name a few. Then they met West Germany in Bloomington (11–3 win) and the Swiss in Minneapolis (11–1 win).

With only one game left on their tournament round-robin schedule, Canada was in the driver's seat. With the Russians out of gold medal contention, the 6-0 Canadians would face 5-1 Czechoslovakia in what would be a de facto gold medal game, which the Canadians needed only to tie in order to clinch their first ever World Juniors gold medal.

It was clear, however, that the IIHF schedule maker had not anticipated the potential gravity of this meeting between Canada and the Czechs. On January 2, 1982—the final day of the U-20 championship—the games involving Russia and the U.S.A. were scheduled for the Met Centre in Bloomington, the NHL home of the old Minnesota North Stars. Switzerland and West Germany were playing the same day in Mankato, at Minnesota State University.

The Canadians and Czechs, meanwhile, were scheduled to play 140 kilometres south of the Twin Cities in Rochester, Minnesota. "A typical small-town rink," Mike Moller recalled. "Probably sat, like, twenty-five hundred to three thousand people." There was some talk about changing the schedule, but that's all it turned out to be. Talk.

"I'm so glad it didn't happen," Moller said. "The people of Rochester, Minnesota, were getting one game—that's all they got. And the whole town was excited about having this game. It was their game."

The Canadians had played five of their six games in NHL arenas. Now it was back to their roots: a small-town, community rink.

"All of us grew up playing in rinks just like this one, in smaller towns," Moller said. "So we get there, we look at each other and say, 'Okay, it's a bit of a smaller rink. Oh, the benches aren't very big. Hmm, neither are the dressing rooms. But, boy, the ice looks pretty good. . . .'

"As a hockey player, what matters more? The ice was great!"

OHL commissioner Dave Branch came down for the game.

"I was with Jim Gregory, and we rented a car together to drive from Minneapolis to Rochester," Branch said. "There was a big snowstorm, and I remember saying, 'Hey, Jim. Do you think anybody back home even knows this game is taking place?' "

At least the media was there, though. Well, some of them, at least. CBC producer Fred Walker convinced his bosses that perhaps he should swing into Minnesota to cover Dave King's team heading for a de facto gold medal game against the Czechs in tiny Rochester.

They got the okay from Mothercorp, so Walker, play-by-play man

Gerry Fogarty, and a technical producer flew into Minneapolis, then drove through the snow to Rochester to call the game on CBC Radio. When the trio arrived, they took organizers completely by surprise.

"They had no idea who the hell we were when we got there, even though we'd asked for credentials before arriving," Walker said. "Then we got into the building, and there was no press box. No place to broadcast from. So they set up some scaffolding at one end of the rink, in the corner. And they set us on top of that, above the glass, sitting ducks for any pucks that came our way."

While the media set up for the game, Sherry Bassin and Bob Strumm, a couple of junior hockey lifers who were involved in the 1982 team's management circle, pulled a stunt that players from that '82 team still talk about. Bassin has run out of motivational ideas and asked Strumm what he could say to the players before the big game.

Strumm paused. "What if I can get you a gold medal?" he asked.

Strumm tracked down a tournament official and asked for a gold medal before the game. Of course, this was not accepted protocol, and the official wasn't sure.

Strumm remembered saying to the man, " 'You want those Commies from Czechoslovakia to win the gold medal? Or do you want to see a bunch of nice Canadian kids win it?' He looked at me and said, 'Meet me in the Zamboni room at six-thirty. I'll see what I can do.'

"So I'm standing in the Zamboni room, colder than hell, and this guy walks by me at about six-thirty, and he drops something in my pocket. It was as big as a hamburger, man. A big, gold hamburger."

Strumm delivered the medal to Bassin, who, Strumm admitted, "was the king of pregame speech-makers."

King echoed Strumm's take. "Bassin told the kids, 'You can look at it, but don't touch it. You have to win it to get your hands on this.' "

It seemed to take a while for Bassin's message to set in, though.

When the game began, it was one-sided—in the Czechoslovaks' favour. Canada trailed 2–1 after forty minutes, with goalie Mike Moffat playing his rear end off, waiting for his teammates to take the game back from Jiří Dudáček, Vladimír Růžička, and the surprising Czechoslovaks, who needed to win in regulation (there was no overtime back then) to finish first and win gold.

Canada tied the game in the third period on a goal by Marc Habscheid. Then Moller snuck one five-hole to make it 3–2 for Canada, a goal he'd never forget.

"There was a line change going on, and [Todd] Strueby and Carey Wilson were still on the ice. Strueby had the puck and was going behind the net, so I just went to the net. It was a bang-bang play, where he shovels it in front of the net to me, and I've got a defenceman on me, and honest to God, I just whack it.

"I'm about ten feet out and I just whack it toward the goal, and the goalie—who is coming off the post to face me—what opens up? The wickets. It just goes right through him and into the back of the net."

Moller and Habscheid were deployed on a line with Scott Arniel, and they were trusted by King to start every period in the tournament. They would account for 16 goals that Christmas, each finishing inside the top seven in tournament scoring.

But it wasn't over. Moments after Moller's go-ahead goal, the Czechs tied it up, and as the clock ticked down, Canada was clinging to their tie—all they required to win gold. At one point inside the final few minutes, Canada lost a face-off in their own end and it resulted in a tough save for Moffat. Now, with their gold medal on the line, and only seconds left on the clock, King was surveying his charges, looking for an answer in the face-off circle.

"Kinger, he looked at the bench, and he found me," Murray said. "Our eyes met, and he goes, 'Go take the draw.' I remember thinking,

'Man, I'd better go win this draw.' They'd been really pressing, and we had to just hang on and not allow that last goal."

King didn't remember it as a split-second decision, even if it appeared that way to Murray. "George, Sherry, and I agreed, if we had a big face-off, Troy would be our guy. He'd find a way to win it."

Murray won the draw and sent it back into the corner. "We scrambled around and were able to get [to the buzzer]," Murray said. "It was chaotic at the end. They were really pushing, and Mike Moffat was really, really good."

The horn sounded in that little, off-Broadway rink in Rochester, and just like that, Canada had its first-ever World Juniors gold medal. But what happened next would become this team's legacy, a facet of the 1982 victory that has lived on long after the names of the players have faded into the mists of World Juniors lore.

"Once all the celebrating was done on the ice, all these sweaty hugs, the high-fives, we're standing on the blue-line, and we're waiting for our national anthem—'O Canada,'" Moller said. "But, it's not coming. They lower the flags, and the fans are ready. Everybody's ready! But it's not coming."

It is international hockey tradition to play the anthem of the winning team after the game. But the game had ended in a tie. Today, it's a given that the gold medal–winning country gets to hear their anthem at the conclusion of the tournament. But in 1982, Canada had never won, and nobody was 100 percent sure what was supposed to happen next.

Moller grinned at the memory. "Kinger and the coaches were like, 'Let's go, boys. Let's get in the dressing room.' And we're like, 'No, no, no, no. We're not going anywhere until we hear the national anthem.'

"And Kinger says, 'It's not coming. So let's get off the ice.'"

But the Canadians weren't going anywhere. Instead, they took matters into their own hands.

"Within two bars we all started singing. . . . Well, yelling it," Moller said. "It was an awful rendition of the anthem. One of the best ones I've ever been a part of. We've got Pierre Rioux, and he's singing in French. We've got guys who are behind a bar or two, so it sounds like an echo. By the end, we are just yelling it out.

"Thank goodness there were a few of us who knew the words."

Even Dave King and the coaches joined in.

"You're damned right I sang. I've got a beautiful voice!" King recalled. "I remember singing with them. It was so, so emotional. The guys had really come together."

It was, in the end, an unfathomable level of success considering the infancy of the Program of Excellence. No one had seriously considered the possibility that Canada could win it all—from the competing teams, to the media who barely acknowledged the event, to whoever was in charge of bringing a tape of "O Canada" to the rink in Rochester.

In fact, some were hoping that the entire concept would fail.

"Winning the gold that first time made the program. Everyone was watching for us to fall on our faces, and we never did. We just got stronger," said Dennis McDonald, who admitted that what happened was beyond his wildest dreams. "It was a desire, a hope. When it happened, it was like our dreams had all come true."

That the very first year of the Program of Excellence could produce a roster that would not only beat the Soviets 7–0 but go on to win a gold medal presented different epiphanies for different people. The doubters were forced to take another look at their stance, especially when the kids rejoined their junior teams to the identical level of fanfare that Costello had predicted back at the Skyline Hotel in

Ottawa. And those who had allowed themselves to believe this idea had some legs, well, they would shake their heads at the unexpected pace of progress.

But for Costello, McDonald, and the commissioners who had signed off on this project, the 1982 team became a foundation. It was on the shoulders of this team that the future of the Program of Excellence would rest, and if this much could be accomplished on the first try, who knew what this program could accomplish in the next decade?

"Everyone who was involved, walking on broken glass trying to sell that program, you've got to give them credit," King said. "The guys went back to their club teams after the tournament, like the Moller brothers in Lethbridge. When they played in Medicine Hat, there was a special ceremony—in Medicine Hat! Everyone was honouring these kids, whether they were on their team or not. The crowd would give them a standing ovation.

"Suddenly, I think, the junior [operators] recognized that this was something that could be really important to them to market their game as the best junior hockey league in the world. That's when some of them saw that this concept had some real potential to help them keep their franchises alive.

"And of course, after 1982, there were no junior players saying they didn't want to play. They all wanted to play."

CHAPTER 3

The Punch-Up in Piestany

"We were not adults, but we were also not innocents."

—BRENDAN SHANAHAN

To really grasp what happened in Piestany, you first have to understand who we were as Canadian hockey people back in 1987; the culture we'd amassed, back when fighting was still a regular, unquestioned occurrence in hockey. When teams would take separate warm-ups in the Western Hockey League because the pregame brawls between teenagers were so frequent.

Canadians like to say that hockey is the ultimate team game. That, unlike basketball where three star players can play nearly every minute in a game and virtually decide its outcome on their own, in hockey, "It takes all twenty guys."

How many times have you heard those five words spoken: "It takes all twenty guys"? That we include the backup goalie in that total, and the fourth-liner who plays six minutes, is testimony to how the team concept has somehow taken hold of this sport more than any of its North American kin.

Like us or not, that is who we hockey people are and how we think. It's why an NHL player can score four goals on a Saturday night and then drone on to Scott Oake about his linemates and the goalie in the postgame interview. Hockey culture dictates that a player should not stand out above his or her teammates. So they certainly won't be seen sitting around idly when a teammate is in trouble.

Still, it had never occurred to anyone on the Canadian side, on January 4, 1987, at the Zimný Štadión Piešťany, that a massive, historic, bench-clearing brawl was even a remote possibility.

"We were prepared for a lot of stuff over there. The food, the schedule, the travel, the systems, the unpredictable refereeing," said Brendan Shanahan, the current president of the Toronto Maple Leafs, who was just seventeen years old at the 1987 World Junior Championships. "But we weren't prepared for that, and I don't think that's anyone's fault."

It *was* someone's fault, however. It was everyone's fault. It was Canadian hockey's fault, for having created a bench full of teenagers who would react like Pavlov's dog the moment two Russians—famously led by former Winnipeg Jets draft pick Evgeny Davydov—hopped over the boards and skated past the Canadian bench en route to a five-on-five melee in the Russian zone.

"What had been drilled into us as hockey players in that era was, you don't let your teammates get outnumbered," Shanahan said.

"It was an instinctual thing," said Team Canada defenceman Luke Richardson, now an assistant coach for the Montreal Canadiens. "And hockey players are always taught to be instinctual. 'Prepare before so you're ready for it, then go on your first instinct.' That was the culture. When two guys went out to outnumber our guys, we were going to even it up right away."

The Punch-Up in Piestany, as it would forever be known, was the fourth and final bench-clearing brawl in Shanahan's junior career. Four "Pier Sixers," as we used to call them—a reference to a bunch of longshoremen brawling on a shipping dock—was likely the average for any player who came though Canadian Major Junior hockey back in his day.

"It seems so crazy and foreign now," Shanahan marvelled. "As it should be."

Richardson? He fought in three such battle royales, all in the 1986–87 season. One earlier in that year, one that day in Czechoslovakia, and . . . well, you won't believe his last one.

"It was my first game coming home, after the brawl in Piestany. A game against Oshawa—our second brawl that season with them. We had quite a rivalry," Richardson said. "Two bench-clearing brawls in two games . . . maybe it was me!"

Truth be told, before the Punch-Up, the 1987 World Junior Championships were not shaping up as even remotely memorable. The host was Piestany, a Slovak town of about twenty-five thousand people living under communist rule in a country then known as Czechoslovakia.

Canada opened with a 6–4 win over Switzerland in nearby Topol'čany, a similarly sized town that had blessed the hockey world with skilled winger Miroslav Šatan. Next, Canada tied Finland 6–6 in

Trencin, and in their third game—when good teams typically begin to find some traction at these tournaments—Canada was stomped 5–1 by the Czechoslovaks.

At 1-1-1, in a round-robin tournament that consisted of just seven games—no playoffs, as there are today—the Canadians had to put together quite a run if their final game, a date with the Russians at the Zimný Štadión Piešťany, was going to have any true meaning.

So Canada went to work, whipping Poland 18–3 in their fourth game, and then solidly thumping Brian Leetch's Americans 6–2 in Game 5. Their sixth game, against Sweden, matched two 3-1-1 teams. Canada beat the Swedes—led by Calle Johansson and Ulf Dahlen—by a 4–3 score.

That should have set up what everyone had expected, and many wanted to see: Canada against the Soviet Union in the final game of the tournament, with everything on the line. But there was a problem.

The Soviets. They were the problem.

"The one thing we didn't expect was a very subpar, and sort of abused Russian hockey team," said Chris Joseph, a defenceman for the Seattle Thunderbirds who wasn't even invited to the summer camp but who made Team Canada at the December tryouts. "The Russians, they were a mess. They weren't very good. They weren't treated well—we were told food was withheld after losses—and they were very poorly managed."

A Soviet Union team that had won gold in each of the first seven IIHF U-20 tournaments from 1974 to 1980, and ten of thirteen WJCs overall, was suffering through its first sub-.500 World Juniors. While everyone else was beating Poland by 10 or more goals, the USSR opened their tournament with a 7–3 win over the Polskas. They predictably beat the Swiss, but lost to Finland, Czechoslovakia, and the U.S., while managing only a tie with Sweden.

It was like watching Tiger Woods miss the cut at Augusta for the first time. The emotions were a mix of confusion and surprise—it just didn't compute that this final game had finally arrived and the USSR hadn't held up their end of the bargain for it to be a gold medal game.

"They were not living up to their mystique," Shanahan said. "They were in fifth or sixth place in the tournament. We were hearing stories about the coaches not feeding them after games, about them being bag skated as punishment. Looking back, they were a tinder box on their own."

The Canadian players, born between late '67 and, in Shanahan's case, early 1969, had grown up in a Canadian hockey culture where the '72 Summit Series was still the starting point of Canada-Russia hockey relations. Back in the seventies and eighties, the Red Army club (CSKA Moscow), as well as teams like Moscow Dynamo or Voskresensk Khimik, would tour through the National Hockey League, with their strange Jofa helmets and almost exclusively left-handed-shooting lineups. They were simultaneously a marvel and a freak show, primitive in their gear yet cutting edge in their style of play.

The older reader will remember a time when the Russians played an emotionless, artistic game that flowed starkly in contrast to ours. The younger reader, unfortunately, has been deprived of an era when a Soviet forward would bring the puck over centre then, not liking what he saw, circle back into his own zone with the puck. His teammates would circle back in his wake, gather as a flock, and forward they would drive again. They were a group of five that could trade the puck like artisans, passing up open shots that our players always took, and waiting instead for the opportunity at a vacated net created by their perfect, deceptive passing.

Then there were their tactics. In those days, the Russian players were under far more serious pressures than their Canadian equals. The Soviet Red Army was exactly that—an arm of the army. Not in terms of fighting wars, but in terms of controlling their players. For instance, Russia would second the best Latvian players, like Helmut Balderis or Sandis Ozolinsh, whether they wanted to come to Moscow to play or not. They'd put their players through an exhaustive summer training camp, keeping them away from their families for months at a time, a practice that eventually led to defections to North America of stars like Slava Fetisov, Igor Larionov, and Sergei Makarov.

On the ice, a Russian player once told me that of a Soviet team, "the most dangerous player at practice is the one who is out of the lineup." A player might literally injure a teammate to open up a roster spot for himself. On the ice, it was a common occurrence for a Soviet player to spit in the face of an opponent to gain an advantage, something that would have serious, painful repercussions in Canadian hockey.

In 1987, even though the Russians had a skilled lineup that included Alexander Mogilny, Sergei Fedorov, Vladimir Konstantinov, Vladimir Malakhov, and Valeri Zelepukin—a group that would combine to play almost four thousand NHL games—the Canadians did not have a clue who they were.

"No social media. Not a whole lot of discussion on who these guys were—certainly not about the players we were playing against," Shanahan said. "That's one of the biggest differences. You go to that tournament now, and not only are some of the Swedes, the Russians, the Czechs your own teammates in the CHL, you have a book on them all. You might even follow them on Instagram, and they might follow you.

"We didn't know who Fedorov was. We didn't know who Konstantinov, or Malakhov, or Mogilny were. We didn't know any of them. Back then, we didn't even know most of our teammates [when training camp opened]."

The Canadians did know one thing, though.

"They were still Soviets. They were still communist," Richardson said. "The Cold War meant it was Russia versus the World. They're like machines out there—they don't show emotion, so it's hard to get a gauge on them, what you're playing against."

Shanahan would spend seven seasons as a teammate of Sergei Fedorov in Detroit, and they talked through the Piestany experience together. Fedorov spoke of the threats the Russian coaches had made against their players, and the air of impending punishment that hung over the players in what remains the worst Russian performance to date at a World Juniors.

"They were being told they had humiliated their country, and their program, and they were all going to be in a lot of trouble. And this was before the game," Shanahan said.

"They were playing like a team that was disgraced," Richardson added. "And they were going to take a piece of something home with them. Unfortunately, that was us."

In effect, the Russians had nothing to lose.

Canada, on the other hand, had everything to gain. Despite having an identical record, the Finns had outscored Canada during the tournament, so Canada had to beat the Soviets by five goals to claim the gold medal. A win by fewer than five, or a tie, and Canada would get silver. They were guaranteed bronze, even if they lost.

Canada was well equipped to rout the Soviets for two reasons:

The Canadians were a very good team, and the Soviets were a defeated group.

"At that time we had a big, strong, fast, physical Canadian hockey team," Joseph said. "Nobody thought that fighting was an issue. We knew we weren't going there to fight, but we were going to play a typical Canadian style of hockey. We were going to play hard and fast and physical."

The referee assigned to the game was one Hans Ivar Ronning of Norway, an official whose experience did not come close to matching the level of vitriol that would meet him in this game. Hockey had not yet graduated to the two-referee system, so this would be Ronning's baby.

That particular assignment, we know now, was one of several poor decisions that would serve as ingredients to the cauldron that was Canada-Russia in Piestany. The game would feature a moment of silence in memory of the four young men—the Four Broncos—who had died five days earlier when the Swift Current Broncos bus crashed on an icy Saskatchewan highway. In a spot of tragic irony, Joseph would lose his son, Jaxon, some thirty-one years later, when the Humboldt Broncos bus crash occurred on the way to a playoff game in Nipawin.

That tribute to the Swift Current Broncos was the end to any human kindness on that January day in Piestany, in a game that would set an unmatched standard for violence at a World Junior Championship.

"It was the perfect storm," Joseph said. "We had a hard, fast game—and the Russians were still fast—but we had three officials who couldn't keep up. So they let incident one go. They let incident two go. They let three, four, and five go. . . . Because they couldn't keep up to the speed or the feel of the game. So one thing turned into another.

"It was like two boys walking down the street. One punches the other in the arm, and the other punches back a little harder. Then next thing you know, you're down on the ground wrestling."

Now, the Canadians, as Shanahan suggested, "were not innocents." Earlier in the tournament, when an American player had skated over the centre line in warmups, the Canadians had lashed out. A skirmish ensued, but again, this was Canadian hockey culture. Every one of these players was raised in the game to know that, if an opponent skated across the centre line in warmups, it was a test of your resolve. If you didn't respond physically, you'd already lost an important part of the game before it had even started.

That is how Canadian hockey players think, both then and, to a lesser extent, now. In fact, when Everett Sanipass started the first actual fight in that game, it was, he said after the game, "to settle things down." You see, in Canada, when the stick work became too sharp or the late hits too cheap, two tough players would have it out. It became the outlet for violence, after which the rest of the two rosters could get back to playing hockey.

Our system worked—or, at least *we* thought it worked. This game, however, wasn't like the games we knew. And this brawl wasn't like any other brawl either. There was no code, no tradition in this brawl.

"There was a way in which these brawls all went down [in North America]," Shanahan explained, "where ninety percent of the guys didn't really engage. If it were Detroit playing Toronto, say, then Steve Yzerman grabbed Vincent Damphousse, and they just stood there and talked while a few guys were combatants.

"The Russians did not know that. So, while a Glen Wesley, or a Pierre Turgeon, or a Pat Elyniuk would engage with someone their size, with their gloves on, the Russians didn't understand that not fighting was an option. That's how it became, like, everybody."

Now, you should know: Neither Richardson, nor Shanahan, nor Joseph—who was on the ice and throwing punches in the second altercation after Sanipass's fight—was looking to pair off passively. Each knew his role was to be a combatant. To be involved.

But other players—ones who would never have to drop the gloves back home—suddenly found themselves fighting in Piestany. "Unfortunately, some of our guys got their asses handed to them by some pretty tough customers from Russia," Shanahan admitted.

A few of the Russian players fought with their gloves on, Richardson said. He recalled falling on top of a player, who then tried to kick Richardson off him using his skates.

"I could feel the skates go by either ear," Richardson said. "I pulled myself in close, and just tried to bear hug him until I felt like I could get up without taking a skate in the face. That's fear, right? He'd probably never been in a hockey fight, coming from his culture, and he didn't feel good about being on the bottom."

At one point, Richardson was distracted by something happening in front of the Soviet bench, "and a guy hoofed me right in the balls."

"Then, I was mad," he said. "I wasn't really mad at the beginning, but I was then."

Joseph was likely the most confused. He was never a fighter to the extent that Shanahan or Richardson was, but he found himself in a scrap near the Russian blue-line. He can still walk through that day in Piestany, almost step by step, with amazing accuracy.

"The game got chippy fast," Joseph said. "We were up 4–2 halfway through the second period, and when the incident happened—and I think it was a stick or a spear or something—it had literally been the fifteenth incident of the game by that time. It was a very ugly game.

"I don't remember who stuck who, but right away somebody took a swing at me, and I grabbed him. We started rolling around on the ice and I was hitting him on the helmet with my glove on. I wasn't hurting the guy.

"I didn't realize that, at the same time, there were four other fights going on. I didn't even know it. I'm engaged. I thought, 'You took the first swing at me,' and I've got this fight going on. All of the sudden I look up, and I've got both benches coming."

Joseph, who had wisely freed his Russian combatant when he saw the benches empty, then went for a skate. Up near the blue-line and past Stephane Roy, Patrick's younger brother, then down near the goalies, who were rolling around in what Joseph recalled as "a comical fight." He pulled a Russian player who'd jumped on top off the pile. "We squared off, I put my dukes up, but nothing happened.

"I didn't get in another fight for a while. And I say a while? It was probably about twenty or thirty seconds from the time I let the first Russian go to the time I engaged in the next one."

The next one was when Joseph spotted teammate Yvon Corriveau.

"One Russian was holding his arms back, and the other Russian was punching him. I skated in and grabbed one of the Russians the same way he had been grabbing Yvon. I've got his arms pinned back, and the other Russian takes off. Now it's me and Yvon, two-on-one against a Russian.

"Yvon's nickname was 'Chachee.' So I yell, 'Hit him, Chachee! Hit him!' Yvon was exhausted, he looks at me holding the Russian's arms back, he looks at the Russian, slumps his shoulders, and goes, 'No . . .' And he skated away."

It's hard to imagine what it's like to be involved in something like this today, let alone as a teenager brimming with testosterone. Forty men, all with their fight-or-flight adrenaline glands fully engaged and not nearly enough officials to preside over the various fights occurring all at once. Especially in Piestany, where the inexperienced officiating crew hung around for a while, before simply leaving the ice with the brawl still fully active.

What's it like to be in a hockey brawl?

"It's a little unnerving," Richardson said, a serious understatement. "You've really got to keep your focus on what's right in front of you, because sometimes you hear a big roar from the crowd, and you've got to be careful your head doesn't turn to see what's going on. You get clocked by the guy right in front of you.

"It's different than a one-on-one fight where you're upset, you drop the gloves, you're going to have it out and it's over. Here, sometimes you'll fall on the ground, you'll get back up, and you're either going to continue fighting or you'll mutually agree, 'That's enough. Let's go make sure nobody is in trouble on each of our teams.'

"You don't know the mentality of your opponent in those times. Fear sets in in any kind of fight, and you act differently than you would normally."

Nothing was normal in those hectic few seconds of the fight. But then things took an even crazier turn: The lights went out.

In a country that just did not have any experience with a situation like this, inside a European hockey culture to which bench-clearing brawls were equally foreign, someone—likely the tournament officials, nobody is completely clear on exactly who made the decision—decided it would be a good idea to turn out every light in the arena.

"When I say the lights went out, it wasn't just shadowy darkness, dim, or a little bit dark. I could not see the person I was wrestling with anymore," Shanahan said. "You're in this dark, dark arena, on a cloudy night. You could feel people skating around you, and hear some voices, some English speaking, some Russian. Yelling, screaming.

"When the refs left the ice, and the lights went out, I'll tell you, it was a fight-or-flight moment," he continued. "I was engaged with a guy, wrestling with him when the lights went out. In as polite a way as possible, I neutralized my opponent at that point. Then I laid on top of him until the lights came back on."

"Everything goes dark," Joseph said. "Then, after a while you can start to tell light and dark colours. It went pitch black for about five seconds, and then you could start to tell red versus white. We were white.

"I was exhausted, I was tired. I wanted peace at this point, so I was mostly going around trying to break stuff up. But there were guys going around suckering guys who were wearing a red jersey."

The darkened arena unleashed a whole new level of fear and aggression.

"They were mad; our guys were mad, too," Joseph said. "We felt like we hadn't had any justice the whole game through and this was our time to let loose—not even thinking about getting suspended."

Again, fear led the way. Almost all of these Canadians had been inside a brawl or two before, but nobody had ever experienced one under these protocols, or lack thereof.

"You could hear the skates in the dark, guys fighting, and chewing up the ice," Richardson said. "That was really scary."

"I always thought when they turned the lights out," Shanahan said, "they were saying to us, 'You little brats. Whatever you've got to do, end this thing.' And when they came back on, it was mostly over."

Back home, when a bench-clearing brawl broke out, the referee would pull out a pen and notepad, travel around through the various bouts jotting down names and numbers, and when the dust settled, he'd toss the three or four main combatants from each team out of the game. Then they'd drop the puck and play on.

The Canadians went ahead on this assumption. The Canadian

game had taught these kids certain tenets, and that was how they understood the game to be.

But it wasn't that way in Piestany.

When everything finally settled down, the officials gathered the equipment in two makeshift piles and sent the players to their dressing rooms. "We all went peacefully," Joseph recalled. "We were done."

But the fun was just starting for Dennis McDonald, who was representing the Canadian Amateur Hockey Association as the administrative point person for the team. The IIHF president, Dr. Gunther Sabetzky, was sour when he called an emergency meeting of the Tournament Directorate, consisting of a delegate from each team plus one from the Host Committee.

"Sabetzky came in and spoke in no uncertain terms about how the whole thing had spoiled the event. Very quickly he seemed to want a pound of flesh," McDonald said. "The Russians, they were going to have the worst record in their history, so they didn't care which way it went. We obviously cared. But every other team in the tournament would improve their position in the standings by the way they voted.

"Even the two teams that were going to be relegated to the B Pool, they would finish ahead of Canada and Russia if we were thrown out, and they'd get another year in the A Pool."

Canada voted against expulsion, of course. The U.S. abstained as a show of solidarity with Canada. But in a meeting that McDonald remembers as taking no more than forty minutes, everyone else voted to punt the Canadians and Russians out of the tournament.

The Canadians would receive no medal of any kind, nor would they be eligible for any awards. "They said we were welcome at the awards banquet," McDonald said. "We politely declined."

It was McDonald who had to break the news to the Canadians that they had been kicked out. Both they and Russia would have their records at the 1987 WJC expunged.

"For the first few minutes when we get back to the room, we hoot and holler," Joseph said. "Then Dennis McDonald came in the room, and he said, 'We've been disqualified from the tournament.' The initial reaction was shock. Then we had swearing, we had tears, we had silence. Pretty much the gamut of emotions. It took us a while to realize that, hey, this is real."

To this day, some people blame McDonald for allowing the IIHF to kick Canada out, accusing him of not having enough backbone in defending Team Canada's right to their medal. But once Sabetzky convened the Directorate, Canada had been doomed.

"We felt that way at the time," Shanahan said, "but I would say now, looking back, that as much as we were unprepared for that moment, I don't blame a Hockey Canada executive for also not being prepared for that moment. I don't hold any grudges. We created the situation, and we paid the consequences.

"You can't go back to a certain moment in time where things happened quickly, and suddenly impart perspective into the minds of everyone involved. I don't feel ashamed of that team, or those guys, or the moment, or what was done. We did the best we knew at the time, considering the situation.

"We were not adults, but we were also not innocents."

After the game, Canada and the Russians exited opposite ends of the arena, under the intimidating supervision/protection of the Czechoslovakian military.

"As we left the arena, the Czechoslovakian military had basically built a tunnel for us. Like, a procession," Joseph recalled. "Every guard had a machine gun over his shoulder and a leashed German shepherd in his other hand. We weren't going anywhere. We were going straight to the bus."

The team drove to Vienna, then spent the night at the airport before boarding their originally scheduled morning flights back to Canada. They were happy to be going home, but uneasy about what was waiting there for them.

Brian Williams is coming at you live from the CBC studios in Toronto, resplendent in one of those peach-hued CBC blazers of yore as he brings us back from live coverage in Piestany. Seated on a comfy couch to Williams's right—no panel desk in those days—a dapper, younger-than-we-remember Don Cherry is decked out in a muted yet clearly expensive grey-toned suit.

It is a Sunday afternoon in January of 1987, and Williams takes the broadcast from CBC reporter Fred Walker, who is on location in Piestany. Before three seconds have passed—prior, even, to Williams's introducing Cherry—the term "black mark for hockey" spills from Williams's lips. Cherry seethes, quietly.

This was the 1987 version of a "hot take," a live, on-camera reaction just moments after the Piestany brawl ended. The CBC gave us Williams, whose resume covering international sports of every stripe is unmatched, and Cherry, whose gaze strayed from Canadian hockey only when he was talking about his beloved bull terrier, Blue. The moment Williams uses those two words—"black" and "mark"—Cherry, his legs comfortably crossed to convey he has seen significantly worse brawls than this little junior tiff, fidgets.

Cherry is hearing Williams talk, but his body language doesn't lead anyone to believe he's really listening. Or more accurately, that he feels the need to hear a pacifist, self-righteous CBC broadcaster crucifying our "good Canadian boys." Even though that's not really what Williams was doing.

Cherry can't wait to tell Canadians how it *really* is, but he speaks calmly as he begins, decrying the fact there was "a lot of kicking going on" in the brawl. "The one thing we don't do," he said, not even bothering to finish his sentence—everyone knows a Canadian hockey player doesn't kick anyone in a bench-clearing brawl. We have brawl protocol in Canada, something no other country can claim. Maybe that should have told us something.

"You know whose fault it's going to be," Cherry warned Williams, and by extension, Canadians. "It's not going to be the Russians' fault. It's not going to be the U.S.A.'s fault. It's always Canada.

"The papers tomorrow, I can see 'Black Mark For Canada.' No matter how good we play, they'll jump all over it. It will be absolutely beautiful," he said, his voice rising in that signature Cherry style, "how it's *always our fault*."

We did not know how it would unfold—nor did Cherry and Williams—but the days and weeks following Piestany would turn into a period of national reflection on how we wanted Canadian hockey to proceed. Canadians debated at length in those early months of 1987 about why we'd come to accept fighting in hockey the way we had.

How was it that a sports system in a country whose apologetic citizens lead NATO in proclaiming "I'm sorry" had come to produce teenagers whose natural response to a difficult situation was to hop over the boards and brawl like animals?

Piestany was entirely organic. That's what gave some people pause. We knew the Canadian kids fought because it was a learned response, not because they were a particularly violent group of players. That under those circumstances, it was the accepted course of action. Most logical Canadians weren't blaming the kids. Williams certainly wasn't.

This had become a seminal moment. An important intersection in Canadian hockey culture, where "old-time hockey" ran smack into a populace that had finally decided to question why our young men were being thrown out of a tournament for bare-knuckle brawling. A growing number of people were no longer comfortable with our favourite sport playing out as if it were in some swinging-doors bar in an old Western movie, especially when it was our youngest who were being exploited.

Just over a decade after the Broad Street Bullies had bludgeoned their way to two Stanley Cups in 1974 and '75—the latter being the last and likely final Stanley Cup ever won by a roster that was 100 percent Canadian—the time had come to re-examine how and why this relic of Canadiana, the bench-clearing brawl, still existed.

In 1987, CBC's *Sports Weekend* was alone on the Canadian TV landscape on a Sunday afternoon in January, and as word spread through the country about the brawl, Canadians tuned to Mothercorp for news on the brawl, and, one hoped, some replays. On that day, at that time, the CBC was the only place that news of this mythical brawl could be found.

"They should all be thrown out of this tournament because the rules of international hockey are very, very clear. There is no fighting," Williams instructed. He blamed Canada and Russia equally and fully endorsed the decision of the IIHF Directorate to expel both teams from the tournament.

Cherry looked at Williams with a knowing grin, stopping short of staring straight into the camera and mocking his host. He was happy to stand alone in defence of our players, our values, and our game. It was right in Don Cherry's wheelhouse.

On that Sunday, the screen shot of Cherry and Williams became our version of the painting *American Gothic*, where the old man and woman stand stone-faced on either side of a pitchfork. There sat Old Canadian Hockey Values in the grey suit, legs crossed on the couch, calmly accepting a huge, violent, turn-out-the-lights brawl. He, like most hockey men, was perplexed that they hadn't just tossed out a few players and continued with the game.

And to his left, clad in a peach-coloured tunic, there was New Canadian Ideals. Williams stripped away tradition, jingoistic pride, and dumb courage—all of the antiquated values that had led us to this pivotal moment in our hockey history. He saw this the way someone would who had never witnessed a hockey game before would see it, and he wasn't ashamed to put a voice to this new way of looking at hockey.

"I don't care who went over the boards first," Williams exclaimed. "We talk about the feelings of these young men. Well, these young men had better learn, and learn quickly, that you don't go through life conducting Pier 6 brawls."

From Cherry's perspective, the Russians had suckered our boys. The Commies had nothing to lose because of their 2-3-1 record, and they'd slashed, speared, and goaded the Canadians into what had resulted. "They're smart," Cherry said. "They know what really gets under a Canadian's skin."

"We do not accept high sticks or spears in the back," Cherry continued. "It's our Canadian nature not to take that stuff. They were the first off the bench, and we fell right into it."

Cherry was not wrong. In fact, his commentary accurately depicted what most Canadians like about the players we produce. But then Cherry had something else to say to Canadians. As the director switched from a "two-shot," with both men on the TV screen, to a "one-shot," a close-up on Cherry, you could catch him taking a quick look to see which camera had the red light on, indicating whether he was alone on the TV screen.

Then Don Cherry turned his gaze to the cameras, and looked Canadians squarely in the eye.

"You people sittin' at home in your living rooms, havin' it all nice and quiet. Maybe havin' a pop or two, or a sandwich or something. You don't know what they've been through over there, and what they're goin' through," he said. "So don't say it's a black mark against our players. Please."

As Williams went to commercial, Cherry looked around the studio with an exasperated expression that asked Canadians, "Can you believe we let guys like this on the air? Like, what language is he speaking?"

"We did not understand the significance of the event as it was happening," Williams said, some thirty-two years later. "It was live television. I was a journalist. You had to have an opinion, and mine was that it was a black mark for hockey. Not for Canada, but for hockey.

"The old joke was, you go to a boxing match and a hockey game breaks out. Well, I didn't like that reputation for our national sport, and it just seemed to me a bad incident. And Don represented the traditional values."

To Cherry's eternal credit, in over thirty years, he hasn't strayed from the beliefs he held that Sunday afternoon in 1987. He still blames the Russians wholeheartedly and believes to his core that they never would have started the brawl had they not been out of medal contention. It was a tactic, and a dirty one at that, because it preyed upon those visceral qualities inside the Canadian hockey player that Cherry—and he's not alone here—values most highly.

While you may have seen a violent, bench-clearing brawl in the tapestry that was Piestany, the only picture Cherry ever saw was a bunch of Canadians protecting each other. Standing up for each other. Having each other's back.

So the fact that we were really the only culture that took things that far meant different things to different people. Pacifists plainly saw a problem with the belief system; a fatal flaw in the stream of inherited knowledge inside Canadian hockey. Loyalists saw Canadians as the hockey culture with the strongest bonds, full of players willing to go to the greatest risks to protect our own.

The Canadian hockey players had conducted a risk assessment that lasted about two-thirds of a second and then made a team decision with little or no group consultation. This was proof for Cherry that Canadian hockey players were born with these qualities. That when it became a choice between flight or fight, a good Kingston boy chose fight over flight every time.

But let's go back. In fact, it was a bit of happenstance that Cherry even ventured into the studio that day in 1987. Williams had issued an invitation a few days earlier, but Cherry didn't see a place for himself on a junior hockey broadcast, and frankly wasn't that interested in being there. Having not received an answer, Williams called Cherry's wife, Rose, who cajoled her husband into taking the gig.

In 1987, Cherry was not yet the Canadian icon he is today. *Coach's Corner* was in its infancy and would only really take off after the Piestany moment. The retired Boston Bruins head coach went downtown that Sunday on the direction of Rose, as a favour to his old friend Williams, and with a small sense of duty to the CBC, where he was yet to be cemented onto the *Hockey Night in Canada* marquee.

"The Russians knew, for sure, that they couldn't win the gold, right?" Cherry says today. "They knew that if they went on there and jumped six Canadians, that we would jump, too—knowing that Canadians would not allow twenty Russians to go after six Canadians. That's the way we are. If twenty guys jump six guys, they deserve what they get."

Once again, more than thirty years later, Cherry's unmistakable voice rises to a crescendo at the end of the sentence: "They deserve what *they* get!"

If there are two things Donald S. Cherry can't stand, it's European players who take advantage of Canadian hockey and the belief system therein, and Canadians who don't live up to those standards by not protecting their own.

"The three guys [the CBC] had over there buried our guys," Cherry said. "I was here with Brian Williams, and naturally he was all about a 'black mark against us' and everything. There's nothing else we could do—as Canadians—when we saw our own players being attacked by the Russians."

Cherry gave no quarter that day. Nor did the uber-polite Williams, who so eloquently stated a position that, somehow, still was misinterpreted by many, including Cherry.

"Sports journalism does not have to be an oxymoron," Williams reminds us. "You can be a journalist without being a homer or a fan."

With that same aplomb today, Williams can view the moment through Cherry's eyes. He sees now that Cherry was setting up as the first line of defence for a bunch of Canadian kids who were coming home to a barrage of criticism; who had taken a deep dive into Canadian hockey morals that they had not created, but had simply acted on.

If Cherry made his point—and, of course, Don makes his point better than most—then the rest of the country would begin to embrace these kids, rather than disown them.

"In 1987, we didn't have the outstanding replays we have today," said Williams, who has done a syndicated radio gig with Cherry for the past thirty-five years. "The angles we have today weren't available. So Don's mentality was, 'I've been over there, I've been speared. I've seen the dirty play. All we want is a chance to face 'em man to man.'

"Don was right. We don't take cheap shots. I believe at the time, and today to some degree, that the proper thing to do is to drop the gloves and fight. Face to face, man to man. You don't attack someone from behind. You don't spear them. I respected Don for that."

This is where Piestany began to usher in some change inside our insular hockey world, however.

Even the most amicable Canadian could differentiate between a clean, hard body check and a sneaky spear or slash. Hell, we had Bobby Clarke, who busted Valeri Kharlamov's ankle in the '72 Summit Series with as ill-intended a slash as had ever been delivered. We had done these things ourselves, and given a choice, every Canadian would take a fair fight between two willing combatants over some dirty stickwork.

Piestany, however, showed us that there was a third option. One that we'd not really ever considered:

What if we kept our gloves on and let the officials sort out the penalties? Why did hockey, on so many occasions, end with a sheet of ice littered with helmets, gloves, and sticks? What if, more than a decade after the Broad Street Bullies, we devised a different, less barbaric solution to problem solving on a hockey rink than bare-knuckle fighting like a couple of circus strongmen?

Piestany initiated a long look inward by Canadians, kick-started by Williams's—and later, Michael Farber's—willingness and courage to go on national television and question one of the pillars that propped up Canadian hockey's pretensions.

Internationally, we were viewed in every other social environment or culture as some of the easiest people in the world to get along with. We weren't the Ugly Americans—we just happened to live north of them. But then we picked up our hockey sticks, and suddenly we didn't take any shit from anybody. "Why was that?" Williams and Farber would ask aloud post-Piestany, the very words a form of Hoser heresy to the Bob and Doug McKenzie set.

"Your DNA is what it is, but at the time it struck me as excessive and embarrassing," said Farber, the former *Montreal Gazette* columnist. "My sense at the time was that Canada didn't want to examine its own role in this. You had a very popular, very effective populist in Don Cherry arguing, 'This is Canada. This is what our lads do.' And I was basically playing the heel on this, by saying, 'Wait a minute. Let's look at our own responsibility. What role does Canada have in what was as embarrassing an event in international junior hockey as I can remember?' "

The night after Cherry and Williams appeared onscreen together, Farber opposed Cherry on CBC's *The National*. Farber's mane of longish, wavy hair and full beard made him look like a peacenik next to Cherry's clean-shaven face that screamed establishment. In that interview, Farber mentioned a seldom-recalled point, namely that Canada had got into some trouble in an earlier game at Piestany versus the U.S.A. when an American player had strayed over the centre line during the pregame warm-up.

"I didn't think the team was well controlled, and that's why I put the blame—perhaps too much—on head coach Bert Templeton and his assistant Pat Burns. I put the onus on the coaches for controlling the players," he said.

This was another relatively foreign concept that would be re-evaluated in North American hockey: tying the players' actions directly to their coach. It's not to say a coach was never fined back in the seventies and eighties, but today, if the NHL's Department of Player Safety disciplines a player for instigating a fight in the last five minutes of a game, his head coach receives an automatic $10,000 fine.

That night, Cherry was once again absolving the entire Canadian hockey world of any wrongdoing—particularly Templeton, who was a good friend. But Farber wasn't buying it.

"What role did we have in this? Do we examine it, or do we just say, 'Oh, no. Not our fault,'" said Farber, whose first child, Jérémy, would be born just nineteen days after the Piestany event, perhaps altering the emotional context of how he looked at those Canadian kids.

"I try to look at myself, and it's something I've asked of my kids," Farber says now. "What is my responsibility here? Sometimes it's not necessarily all on you, but you have to look, I think, at what part you played. Essentially, that was my argument. Let's examine our role. Canada's role."

As time passed—after the media storm that met the players coming home to Canadian junior clubs, and after Toronto Maple Leafs owner Harold Ballard invited the team to a game at the old Maple Leaf Gardens and bestowed upon them replacement gold medals—everyone began to go their separate ways.

Cherry's career ascended, even though he'd feared for his job after that original interview with Williams, who saw things quite differently.

"I knew that Canadians, traditionally, are very peaceful people," Cherry said. "And to have gone on television and said that the players should have gone on [to the ice] and attacked the Russians. . . . I thought I was finished, for sure. I was told as I walked out, by a white-haired gentleman who was the senior producer of CBC Sports, that I was finished on television.

"My wife—who was my worst critic—she thought I was right. And I think the rest of Canada did, too."

Well, not necessarily the rest of Canada.

History records that Canadian defenceman Luke Richardson's very first game back with the Peterborough Petes after returning from Piestany was marred by a bench-clearing brawl. And on February 26, 1987, at the Boston Garden, the Bruins and Nordiques would engage in what would become known—at least, to the date of this writing—as the last ever bench-clearing brawl in the history of the National Hockey League. The game featured eight game misconducts by such luminaries as Gord Donnelly, Ken Linseman, Dwight Foster, and Basil McRae, as the Nords and Bruins racked up 231 penalty minutes between them.

It wasn't that this particular brawl was worse than any other. It just came at the right moment for history to record it as the NHL's final bench-clearing brawl—not two months after Piestany, and a couple of months before the May 14, 1987, pregame playoff melee between the Philadelphia Flyers and the Montreal Canadiens at the Montreal Forum.

Following that sequence of events, the NHL enacted Rule 70.1, Fines and Suspensions. It stated that the first player to leave the bench for the purpose of starting a brawl would receive an automatic ten-game suspension without pay—regular season or playoffs. Everyone else who left the benches would get a five-game ban, and the head coach would be levied a $10,000 fine.

To Farber and Williams, this was the sort of thing we were ready for. Canada was ready to move past the vulgar brutality that was twenty-on-twenty, bare-knuckle brawling. Canadians just needed something—a moment, an occurrence of significant relevance—to get the conversation rolling.

Through the combined forces of Cherry, Williams, and Farber, Piestany had become exactly that.

"It was such a cathartic event that it demanded a visceral response," Farber said. "On some level, it was almost a Rorschach test—you had to respond in some way. You could not be ambivalent.

"You could look at Jordan Eberle's goal, and you could cheer it . . . or not. It didn't demand a response. 'Maybe I'm not interested in junior hockey.' But this? It needed a response.

"I moved to Montreal in '79," he said in conclusion, "and one of the first things you heard was if the Canadiens were fighting on a Saturday, then there will be a fight at every rink in town on Sunday morning. That was the template."

On the Monday that Farber was readying to take on Cherry on the CBC, Williams flew to San Diego for a conference. He'd heard of the ruckus back home, and late that afternoon he rung up his old friend Don.

"I called the house and Rose picked up the phone," Williams recalled. "She said, 'Don, it's Brian. You know how sensitive he is.' So Don picks up the phone and he says, 'Hello, Comrade!'"

Williams laughed.

"A couple of weeks later he's speaking to a Lions Club, as a favour to me. He looks out over his audience, and says, 'It's nice to see Brian here tonight. I knew he was here because his Lada is parked right next to the front door.'"

In the end, Williams was right: Piestany was a black mark. But it was probably inevitable, to some extent. In the ensuing years, the Canadian game would become more nimble and less rooted in traditional reactions. We would coach our young players for what was to come in a particular game, not by what had transpired over decades of Canadian hockey.

Our coaches would become the leaders we expect them to be. Men who taught young players how to deal with adversity with their gloves still on. And the old days? They began to disappear.

CHAPTER 4

Coaching, Chemistry, and Character

"Whether you're talking about your elite player or your thirteenth forward, one of the things we looked at first and foremost was character."

—PERRY PEARN

The question came, *en français*, from within a group of Canadian reporters. Something about the unique challenges Canada faced when preparing to play against a weaker team like Germany.

"Anybody want to translate that for me?" said Brent Sutter, a farm boy from Viking, Alberta.

"You don't speak French?" the reporter asked in French.

"Anyone want to translate *that* for me?" Sutter repeated.

There is being a hockey coach, which means picking a team in

September, growing with it through the season, ideally taking it into the playoffs in the spring, and riding your work as far as it will take you. Then there is being a World Juniors hockey coach, where that nine-month process is compacted inside about an eighteen-day window.

Throw in an unreasonable level of pressure to win from a country that throws around the term "gold or bust"—as though it's that easy to just continually be the best in the world at something—and you start to get an idea of what it's like to coach Team Canada at a World Juniors.

If you talk to any junior coach across Canada, he or she will tell you the same thing: Every day, it's something. A player skipped school or missed a test. A girlfriend problem has cropped up. Something's up at a billet house. Someone's parents want them to come home. Someone's parents are complaining about ice time. Somebody had a fender bender on the way to practice.

Being responsible for twenty-two teenagers is as frenetic as it sounds—and that's if you're coaching a team in Chicoutimi, Guelph, or Moose Jaw. Now, try it behind the Iron Curtain, in 1988 Moscow, just twelve months after Canada and Russia had come together for the shameful exercise that was the Punch-Up in Piestany.

Cold War Moscow. Not exactly the greatest place for a field trip.

"What did we learn as young kids in school growing up?" said Sheldon Kennedy, who played on that 1988 Team Canada. Kennedy was born in 1969 and grew up in tiny Elkhorn, Manitoba. "We learned about the Cold War. The KGB. 'Be careful of the Russians, in case their nukes come over. Get under your desks, kids!' I remember the build-up and animosity, when the Red Army team came over to play Canada. Those were huge games. Canada Cups, all that stuff."

The IIHF had originally planned to ban Canada and Russia for a year after Piestany, until it was pointed out that the 1988 World Juniors were set for Moscow, and it would likely help the gate to have a home team in the tournament.

Ken Hitchcock was an assistant coach on that 1988 team, alongside Jean Begin and head coach Dave "Doc" Chambers. Between the communists, the fall out from Piestany, and the fact the Soviets were under even more pressure to win that year—being at home in Moscow—there was a lot in play for a coach/chaperone at the 1988 WJC.

"The pressure on this team from above was incredible. Not coming from Hockey Canada, but from government people, nationally, to behave ourselves, because the year before was a mess," Hitchcock said.

"[CAHA President] Murray Costello had to do a lot of work just to get us back in the tournament, so we weren't suspended. There were a lot of people involved in that, and the government people were around us in training camp.

"Also, news of that incident was really widespread in Europe—even more so than in Canada. In Canada, we've seen all that before [brawls and such], in pro and in junior. We just move along. But it was a very, very big deal in Europe."

With the post-Piestany cloud hovering over the program, the coaching staff in 1988 put together a Canadian team heavy on character. There was going to be a lot of adversity and intimidation in Moscow. If the players weren't strong enough mentally, the 1988 Team Canada would be beaten before they even laced up their skates.

On the ice, the Canadians were expecting a double whammy from the officials. It was bad enough for a Canadian playing games inside the legendary Luzhniki Sports Palace, where the physical Canadian style never enjoyed a welcoming embrace, but coming off the bench-clearing brawl the year before, Doc Chambers was fully expectant that Team Canada would be a target for the referees.

"Doc's attitude was, 'You're going to get screwed every day. Things that are acceptable in North America are penalties here, and you're going to have to get used to it,'" Hitchcock said.

Leading up to the tournament, Team Canada trained in Vierumäki, Finland, and spent far more time each practice working on the penalty kill than any Canadian coach had ever seen. "I thought this was a strange way to do business," Hitchcock said. "Then we played an exhibition game in Helsinki and we spent the whole night in the penalty box.

"Dave Chambers, he made killing penalties a part of every pre-game skate, every practice, every day. By the end, we still took penalties, but the team was in such cohesion on the penalty kill it wasn't a big deal. Because Dave spent so much time, with unbelievable detail, and he had us do it from the first day."

But while the coaches could prepare for a certain landscape on the ice—a hockey environment where they could predict what they'd face—off the ice was a whole different bag of pucks. This was still old-time communist Russia, a full three years before the Berlin Wall would come down.

Kennedy's description of what the average nineteen-year-old knew about communist Russia back in 1988 was accurate. It was so foreign to what a Canadian kid's eyes had seen, with soldiers, shady black marketeers, and mysterious figures in hotel lobbies who they simply assumed had ties to—or were eyes for—the KGB.

"You'd go to a shopping mall in Moscow, and the name of the store is, 'Shoes.' Then you look across the way and it's 'Jeans.' That's how they shopped. What a huge eye-opener for us," Kennedy said. "From the time that we landed, [the Russians] were playing games with us. Walking up and down the hallways, ringing our rooms in the middle of the night. The food was never on time and not well done. The bus was always late. I think Joe Sakic lost ten or fifteen pounds over there.

"One of the things that I remember was the Americans at the airport when they arrived. [The Russians] went through every bag and everything that they had. They were in the airport for a full day."

"Our food was stolen," Hitchcock said. "We got phone calls in our rooms four, five, six times a night in the Hotel Russia."

Hockey Canada brought over diplomat Ken Taylor, the former Canadian ambassador to Iran who covertly freed six Americans from the country during the Iran hostage crisis in 1979. "He told us how to act, how to behave," Hitchcock said.

When the tournament began, the coaches had to be prepared for a type of intimidation that was far removed from the kind of intimidation doled out at rinks in places like Prince Albert or the Soo. This was another level from what anyone had encountered in the CHL.

"I remember being on the bench and looking straight across, and there was [Viktor] Tikhonov and the Russian coaching staff," Kennedy said. "They had the long, black coats on, and the fur hats. It was a packed house, Luzhniki arena, and there they were, right at eye level across from our bench. Just sitting there. It was all built on intimidation, such an eye-opener for a kid coming out of little Elkhorn, Manitoba, then Swift Current. Now, suddenly, we're in Moscow, Russia."

Whether or not Tikhonov and his cronies had intended to strike fear into the Canadians, their presence did exactly that. It was just another reminder that they were far from home in a vastly different culture. And the Red Army was watching.

You'll hear Canadian coaches talk about balancing skill and character when putting together a roster for a World Juniors tournament. This particular tournament required a character-heavy lineup, because the pressure that was coming from back home—and from the Soviets—was unprecedented. If the coaches didn't get the chemistry right back in Canada when choosing the team, it didn't matter how smart they were when the bullets started flying. Chambers and his staff were confident they had found the right mix.

"The two guys who shined through in a huge way were Sheldon Kennedy and Theo Fleury," Hitchcock said. "They made fun of every bit of adversity we went through like it was nothing to them. It was amazing watching these two guys operate. . . . It was tough sledding for a lot of people, and those guys, they had a lot to do with the chemistry of the hockey club."

"Most guys were very nervous over there. It was scary," Kennedy said. "What I brought to the table was lightening things up with a joke and keeping people's minds off of the realities with a lot of laughter. Keeping people upbeat. Theo, he brought a lot of the character on the ice. The way he played and the confidence he had that we would win this tournament, it kind of took away the fear and nervousness."

Having the right roster in place helped to offset some of the pressure, but there was another problem: the schedule.

Because both the Soviets and the Canadians had been disqualified the year before in Piestany, they were both seeded as if they were the seventh- and eighth-place teams in an eight-team round-robin. So, Canada opened against Sweden (4–2 win), followed by the Czechs (4–2 win), the Finns (4–4 tie), and the Americans (5–4 win).

Canada was 3-0-1 by the time they met the 4–0 Soviets, and both teams' remaining games would be against West Germany and Poland—neither of which was expected to put up much of a resistance. So when Canada and Russia lined up on New Year's Day,

1988—in the same rink where Paul Henderson had scored sixteen years earlier to win the Summit Series for Canada—it was once again a de facto gold medal game, the culmination not just of the tournament, but of twelve months of politics.

"There was a lot of pressure on us—and the Russians—to win," Kennedy said. "We needed to win, for everything that had happened the year before. But Russia had a powerhouse team that was *supposed* to win."

"In '88 the best line in the tourney was Sergei Fedorov, Alex Mogilny, and Dmitri Khristich," Hitchcock recalled. "That line was about total possession and total regroup. It was my first experience at watching regroups that, for a long time, made no sense to me. When you gain territory, why you take it back out and try to regain the same territory again made no sense to me."

The Russian system was effective, though. Canada was dominated on the shot clock—and we will assume, in Corsi—by the Soviets. The Soviets would outshoot Canada 40–16 in the game, including 17–4 in each of the second and third periods.

"Adam Graves played against Fedorov. It was a matchup for the ages," Hitchcock said. "Doc got Adam out against Fedorov every shift. I remember how good Jimmy Waite was, but Graves, he looked like a man among boys."

Canada would prevail 3–2 then win out against West Germany and Poland, becoming the first team other than the Soviets to win a gold medal at a WJC hosted in Russia. They could not claim that their system prevailed over the way the Soviets played the game, because the USSR had dominated everywhere except the scoreboard. But Canada had overcome a whole lot of intangibles, and plenty of intimidation, real or perceived.

So let's dig in a little bit on systems, because going over to Europe to play teams from seven different countries is a major departure from, say, going to a Memorial Cup and facing three other junior clubs that all play a variation of Canadian hockey.

Perry Pearn is, like Hitchcock and Dave King, a disciple of the coaching tree of Clare Drake, the dean of Canadian university hockey coaches, whose plaque hangs in the Hockey Hall of Fame. Drake coached at the University of Alberta, and although he never worked a World Juniors, he coached Canada's 1980 Olympic team, worked a Spengler Cup, and spoke annually at coaching conferences attended by the various WJC coaches over many years.

"One of the great learning experiences for Hitchcock and myself was being involved in the Under-16 program in Alberta," said Pearn, a WJC assistant coach in 1990 and '91, and the head coach of the gold medal Canadian team in 1993 in Gavle, Sweden. "You'd go do the U-16 and you'd be working with Clare Drake and George Kingston. You couldn't help but learn."

Pearn went on to work twenty-one consecutive seasons as an NHL assistant coach, many alongside Martin in Ottawa and Montreal. Today, Pearn is back with Hockey Canada as the head coach of the Canadian women's national team, having learned much about international hockey during his three World Juniors.

"I remember in '90 in Finland," he said. "One of my jobs was to . . . watch the Russians play. So I had a Finnish driver, and we were situated in Vierumäki, and we went off somewhere into Finland. The roads weren't great, and we arrived just a little bit late. But I got there just in time to be standing on the rail, watching a Russian defenceman go behind their net. They were playing a Finnish Elite League team, and he fired a long pass, one that wasn't on the ice. It was, like, two feet in the air, and it was hard. It almost looked like a slap shot.

"Then I saw this streak of red come across the blue-line, stick his stick in the air, and just tap the puck down to his feet. He went in and scored. It was Bure. And the player who made the pass? It was Sergei Zubov. I was thinking to myself, 'Oh, boy. How the hell are we going to beat these guys?'"

Two years after Hitchcock's experience in Moscow, the Russian hockey system was still clinging to its patient puck-possession game, a system that was nearing extinction in 1990.

"In the nineties there had been minimal players defect from Russia," Pearn said. "They were still playing that puck control system. They would hang on to pucks, take pucks back, and regroup. The passing game that, if you fell sleep against them they would sneak someone in behind you."

The last of the graceful, highly skilled, old school Russians played in those World Juniors from 1988 to 1992, during which time Russia won two golds and three silvers. At the same time, some classic Swedes were plying a different trade for the Tres Kronor—names like Johan Garpenlöv, Ricard Persson, Mats Sundin, Nicklas Lidström, Michael Nylander, and Peter Forsberg.

"The Swedes were way more conscious defensively than even the Finns," Pearn said. "The Finns, the Russians, they played more of a wide open game. They wanted to attack. The Swedes would attack, but they were way more calculated. They played a much more sophisticated defensive system."

The "left-wing lock" was invented by the Czechoslovaks to slow down the talented Big Red Machine of the Russians in the 1970s. In that system, as the opponents exited their zone with the puck, the Czechoslovaks' left-winger would fall back in line with their two defencemen. As the attacking unit moved toward the open ice on the left wing, the Czechoslovak centre and right-winger would swing over, "locking" the puck carrier in a pocket against the boards, where he'd be surrounded by a well-positioned defence and two forwards crashing down from above.

The "left-wing lock" was adopted by the Swedes, who tweaked it a bit, but retained the integrity of its defensive structure. Later, the Neutral Zone Trap was able to defeat the left-wing lock, so the Swedes invented a more aggressive system called the Torpedo, which required a great deal of skating.

"The Torpedo has four people on the attack, but if you're going to play it, you really have to come back hard. It's a more high-tempo game," Pearn said. "In the World Juniors that I was in, the Swedes played more of a left-wing lock. Their neutral zone was real good, and you knew that if you went back in your end to set up you'd be looking at a 1-3-1 look. You were forced to play a bit more of a puck possession game, and if you did chip it in, it had to be a soft chip so the guy chipping it, or maybe a support guy, could be right on top of their defence. Otherwise your forecheck game wasn't effective at all."

European teams, especially then and to a lesser extent today, had the benefit of playing several tournaments as a unit, while Canada only came together once for real games, at Christmas. Today, some of the best European hockey talent plays in the CHL or at North American universities, so they are unavailable to national teams outside the WJC. But the Finns, for instance, have full-time national coaches at the U-17, U-18, and U-20 levels—and a general manager who oversees them all. They run their teams through several European tournaments that give them more experience together. Canadian coaches tend to have less time to install their systems, so they get right to the point.

"The focus on the Canadian teams I worked with was, 'How are we going to play defensively?'" Pearn said. "It wasn't as important to be organized offensively, because you had the best of the best in

Canada. Guys with offensive flairs and skill, and who knew how to play the game that way."

It can become a teaching moment, when you consider that no kid ever went out the door to play street hockey and dreamed of making an important check in a World Juniors game. Or a crucial shot block. It's about scoring goals, and at this age group, with this level of offensive skill, developing the player can be as important as developing the person.

"They're going to be good players. It's getting them to play a certain way for a certain period of time," said Tim Hunter, head coach of the 2019 Team Canada. "Take a simple thing like back tracking, or back checking. It's non-negotiable. Everyone has to do it. With star junior players it's, 'We'll get there when we get there.' They take circuitous routes on the forecheck. Little things that can't work [at the WJC]. That's the part of selling the commitment. I sell it to them as, the more flexible you are as a player here . . . the better opportunity you'll have of becoming a good pro."

Here's an example Hunter uses with his players, both with Team Canada and Moose Jaw, where he coaches full-time:

"Brayden Point: His first World Juniors, he's the thirteenth forward, he's playing on the wing. Next World Juniors, he's the captain and number-one centre. First year pro, he makes Tampa on the wing. Killing penalties. Second-year pro, he's playing centre and he's in the All-Star game. Playing powerplay *and* penalty kill. All because he was willing to be flexible.

"You play the wing, you understand the game better. You kill penalties, you understand the powerplay better."

If players are expected to be flexible, however, so, too, must coaches learn to work with the personality and limitations of the rosters they are given. Any successful Team Canada head coach has managed to successfully read the strengths of his roster and apply those assets to building a style of play that can win at the international level.

Brent Sutter had perhaps two of the most dissimilar rosters possible in 2005 and 2006, the back-to-back years he coached the WJC team. In 2005, it was the Dream Team in North Dakota; the next year, it was a team with one returning player (Cam Barker) in Vancouver. Of course, in 2006 they still had a goalie named Justin Pogge, a seventeen-year-old college kid named Jonathan Toews, an eighteen-year-old Kris Letang on defence, and a bunch of future NHLers like Steve Downie, Andrew Cogliano, Benoit Pouliot, and Blake Comeau up front. But gone were Sidney Crosby, Patrice Bergeron, Shea Weber, and the rest of the future superstars who had won gold in 2005 on what is widely considered to be the best lineup ever sent to a WJC.

"You know, you don't always have to have big-name players to be successful. You can put a team with that junkyard dog mentality, that goes through the wall to be successful," Sutter said. "In '05 you had so much talent. Then you had Jonathan [Toews] in '06. Those two years of coaching World Juniors are years I'll hold to the highest standards, always."

That's as close as you'll ever get to hearing a Sutter say, "I'm proud as hell of the job I did there." But knowing all the Sutter brothers as we do, those words would never pass their lips.

"To me," Anaheim captain and 2005 alum Ryan Getzlaf said, "[Sutter] was a coach who made you feel confident. He never wanted you to get a big head, but he definitely never kicked you or put you down, either. He wanted you to have the confidence to play the game the way we were capable of playing."

In 2014, with the program slipping a bit—between 2010 and 2013 Canada had just a silver and two bronze to show for their efforts—

Hockey Canada CEO Bob Nicholson called Sutter back to the bench. The Program of Excellence was trending downward, and in 2015 and 2017 they were scheduled for a split WJC between Toronto and Montreal.

So Nicholson rang up Sutter, in search of an infusion of some integrity in 2014. Because coaching isn't always about the Xs and Os.

"Bob approached me, and he said, 'We want to get this thing up and running again. On a path where we can have some success again. Maybe change some things internally,'" Sutter recalled. "It wasn't so much coaching the team, but it was about helping Bob with the process of putting the culture back into the place it needed to be put.

"You always want to think you're going to win, and Canada always has an elite team. But our whole focus that year was to be competitive. We knew we were going to be young, but we tried to set it up so that we were making sure we had a lot of players returning when we were hosting it in our country [in 2015]. Our mindset was, 'Boy, if we can medal it would be a great accomplishment.' And we got beat in the bronze medal game. We weren't quite good enough that year, to win that tournament."

The Canadians had played in the smaller rink in Malmö, Sweden, throughout the 2014 tournament, where they were drawing about 3,000 fans per game—many of them Canadians who had travelled over to cheer for their team. Then, for the semifinal against the powerful Finns, Canada moved into the big rink for the first time. "The whole atmosphere was different for our players," Sutter said.

This stuff matters when you're dealing with teenagers. There aren't a lot of tactics in the coaching manual to deal with an atmospheric shift like moving into a 13,000-seat building, one of the largest in Sweden, for a sudden-death game.

"From a 3,500-seat building to a 13,000-seat building," Sutter said. "And in that 3,500-seat building, you had 3,000 Canadian fans. They weren't as noticeable in the big building. The whole atmosphere was completely different. Totally opposite from what it had been.

"We gave it our best, and it wasn't quite good enough."

Marc Habscheid holds the honour of being the first person ever to both play for Canada's World Juniors team and then become its head coach. He was a centre on that 1982 team that linked arms and sang the anthem in Rochester, Minnesota. Then he stepped behind the bench of the 2003 team in Halifax, a team that stole Canadians' hearts to the extent that an average of 1.1 million viewers watched each of the preliminary round games—a TSN record. The gold medal game drew 3.7 million viewers, the largest single-game audience in network history at the time.

"In '82 we had one game televised, and the gold medal game was on CBC Radio," Habscheid recalled. "The biggest difference was, back in '82 there were players who decided not to go. Brent Sutter opted not to play, for instance. Now that never happens. Now they'll do anything to play."

Habscheid was trying to build chemistry in a hurry in '03, so he drew on his experience from two decades before, when head coach Dave King and the CAHA were basically flying by the seat of their pants.

"Dave King was the pioneer, and one of the things I remember about him was we walked into the dressing room at Winnipeg Arena, and he had a shelf there. We came in, and Dave asked everyone to put their egos on that shelf. 'Take your role, accept your role.' That, as a coach, is the most important thing," said Habscheid, who gave Carlo Colaiacovo, Kyle Wellwood, Brooks Laich, and the rest of his players a variation of the same theme twenty-one years later. "You're short-term, and it's about the end product. Ice time isn't important. You'll be remembered for whether you won or you lost. So you have to gather everyone as fast as you can, but it's a short time frame. And you also have to learn about people."

So, how does a coach condense that period of time where he gets to know his players and staff? Habscheid was presented with an opportunity right off the hop, when Hockey Canada came up short on T-shirts.

"We had twenty-two players and about six staff members, but we didn't have enough shirts for everyone," said Habscheid. "So I said 'Everyone get a T-shirt.' And then we watched what happened. Because we knew we were four short.

"Who took one? Who didn't? Who gave one back, to someone else? I needed to learn about our people, and I didn't have much time. I learned a lot," he said. "Some staff took one. Some players gave theirs away. Some wanted to keep theirs. It was just all the little interactions, and you watched them and learned about the people."

Almost every Team Canada coach you speak with tells a tale about a certain player, one who became a focal point during selections, or had to be monitored through the tournament. A "risk and reward" player whose presence could make or break a team inside the short window that is the WJC.

For Habscheid, that player was Jordin Tootoo.

"He was an impactful player because of his physical nature, but now you're playing in a tournament where you have international referees," Habscheid said. "So, there was a lot of talk internally about, how is this going to translate to the international game?"

The other thing with Tootoo was that he was a bit of a wild child. Today he is a recovered alcoholic, retired from the game and living a clean, family-first life. But in 2003, Tootoo was a nineteen-year-old at the most volatile time in his life, having just lost his older brother and mentor, Terence, to a suicide that had devastated Jordin.

Tootoo was fragile, and his game was dangerous. But Habscheid and his assistants brought him on and then began work on keeping Tootoo within the confines of what it took to have a successful team.

"We told him: 'Jordin, these are the boundaries, and you have to stay inside of them, otherwise this could go the other way on us.' In the end, he created the energy, we had the 'Tootoo Train,' and the fans really got behind him," said Habscheid. "When he was on the ice, you could feel the energy, and he finished his hits. He was a legit concern for the other teams."

Tootoo took just two minor penalties in that tournament, and Canadians got to know the Inuit kid who walked into the Program of Excellence through the Brandon Wheat Kings. As Pierre McGuire said, it was quite the love affair that ensued, but one that a kid who grew up hunting seals with his grandfather on the Arctic tundra, then came down to a big city named Brandon, Manitoba, wasn't necessarily ready for.

"He was starstruck, for sure," Habscheid said. "But to be fair, they're all teenagers. They are all outwardly confident, but inside it's a big deal for them. And with Jordin, it wasn't like he was in a city like Edmonton playing minor hockey since he was five years old, and now he's on the national stage. He came from a small place, and he became one of the focal points on our team. . . . All in all, he handled it really well, for the stage that he was on."

For Perry Pearn in Sweden in 1993, his version of a "risk and reward" was of a different vein.

"One of the things Canada was the best at was team building," Pearn began. "We had an ability to get that group of athletes that you pulled

Murray Costello (left) was the architect of the Program of Excellence, along with Dennis McDonald, program director of the Canadian Amateur Hockey Association (CAHA). Costello was president of CAHA from 1979 to 1994 and then its successor, Hockey Canada, from 1994 to 1998.
Hockey Hall of Fame

The 1982 roster was the first Team Canada to come out of the Program of Excellence. They would win it all in Rochester, Minnesota, and when the national anthem failed to play, they would invent the tradition of singing "O Canada."
Hockey Canada Images

Wayne Gretzky playing against the United States during the 1978 World Junior Championship (WJC) in Montreal. To date, no sixteen-year-old has ever scored more than the 17 points Gretzky piled up at that tournament—not Sidney Crosby, Eric Lindros, or even Connor McDavid. *Montreal Gazette/John Mahoney*

The 1987 Punch Up in Piestany. Chris Joseph (No. 5) pulls a Russian player away from teammate Yvon "Chachi" Corriveau. Both Canada and Russia would be disqualified from the tournament, costing Canada its medal. *Associated Press*

Eric Lindros played in three WJCs from 1990 to 1992. His eleventh-hour addition to the 1992 team in Fussen, Germany, caused Hockey Canada to establish a policy that made the December camp mandatory for every player. *The Canadian Press/ Ryan Remiorz*

The 1991 tournament in Saskatchewan marked the arrival of The Sports Network (TSN) and the airing of every Team Canada game. John Slaney scored the tournament-winning goal that year, and Canada would go on to win eight of ten gold medals between 1988 and 1997. *Hockey Canada Images*

Paul Bereswill/Hockey Hall of Fame

Roberto Luongo allows the winning goal in overtime of the 1999 gold-medal game in Winnipeg. "I was crying, everyone was crying after the game," he said. *The Canadian Press/Kevin Frayer*

As the Winnipeg crowd stood in applause after the game, Luongo was consoled by captain Mike Van Ryn and forward Tyler Bouck. *The Canadian Press/Tim Krochak*

Still just seventeen, Sidney Crosby hoists the trophy in 2005 in North Dakota. Assistant captain Patrice Bergeron and Corey Perry were also part of what is acknowledged as the best team ever iced at a WJC.

Dave Sandford/Getty Images

Jordan Eberle tied the 2009 semifinal in the game's dying seconds. "People have asked me so many times about it, I've replayed it so many times," he said. "I always say, I was in the right spot at the right time, and I was able to finish it off." *Richard Wolowicz/Getty Images*

Connor McDavid unleashes a shot at the 2015 WJC. He enjoyed this, his second WJC, much more than the first, winning gold in Toronto and Montreal. *Steve Russell/Getty Images*

Max Domi celebrates a goal in the gold-medal game against Russia at the 2015 WJC. Canada held a 5–1 lead, then hung on to beat the Russians 5–4 in a nail-biter. *Claus Andersen/Getty Images*

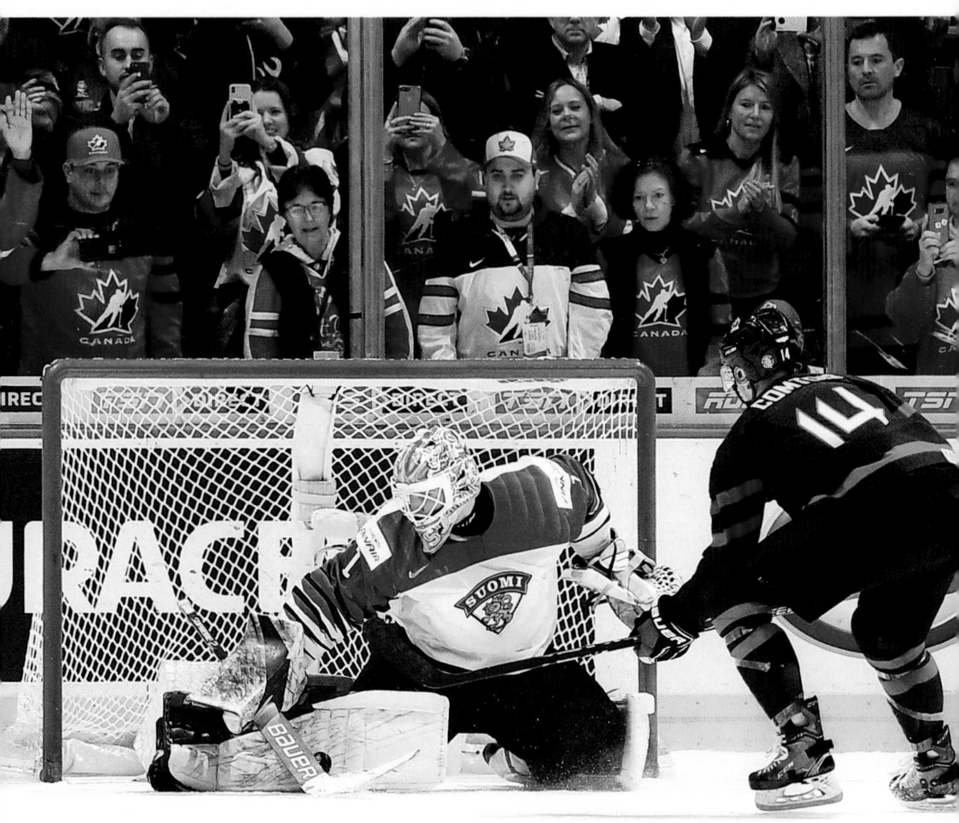

Maxime Comtois is thwarted on a penalty shot in overtime by Finnish goalie Ukko-Pekka Luukkonen. The Finns would score a lucky goal moments later, knocking Canada out in the quarterfinals of the 2019 tournament. *Matt Zambonin/HHOF-IIHF Images*

together from a bunch of different locations, draw them together, and get them to play as a unit in a short period of time. Much better than the Finns or the Swedes—and it turned into a psychological edge.

"We sold, from a Hockey Canada standpoint, that we were more organized, we were better prepared . . . that we were just better. The players believed that, and some of the Europeans saw that, and they thought that, too."

There were times, however, that Canada simply got it all wrong. Hard lessons. Like the 1992 World Juniors in Fussen, Germany.

"The disaster in Fussen?" Bob Nicholson asked.

Yes, the disaster in Fussen. It was one of those experiences you had to live through, then look back upon to realize its impact, and unfortunately for Nicholson, it happened on the first World Juniors that he was in charge.

In 1992, Team Canada had let Eric Lindros and two others miss the December camp and then drop in on the team at the last moment. The controversial move created a sense that those three would come in and save the day, which turned out to be a terrible theme around which to build a successful team.

The CAHA had named Rick Cornacchia as head coach. He was the head coach of the Oshawa Generals, where Eric Lindros was en route to becoming the next generational superstar. Still a junior, Lindros had already joined Wayne Gretzky, Mark Messier, and all the other NHL stars in the 1991 Canada Cup the previous August. As an eighteen-year-old, he had played just thirteen games for Oshawa, then moved on to Canada's national team, which was preparing for the 1992 Olympic Games in Albertville, France.

Goalie Trevor Kidd and defenceman Karl Dykhuis—both still junior-aged—were also on that national team. But it was the Great Lindros who was being talked about that winter by every Canadian hockey fan, as well as everyone involved with that Canadian entry in the 1992 World Juniors.

"I spoke to [national team coach] Dave King twice a day, trying to get them [Lindros, Kidd, and Dykhuis] released to go to World Juniors and not play on the national team, which was preparing for the Olympic Games," Nicholson recalled. "Every time I talked to our coaches, they were like, 'Are they coming?' We didn't care when they got there. They could have pulled in ten minutes before the first game."

The trio would arrive a couple of days before the tournament began, fashionably tardy and too late to have had any involvement in the pretournament selection camp. "He was the saviour," said Nicholson of the perception surrounding Lindros's arrival. "In the end, we didn't play bad, but we didn't have the focus on the team. We came home, and I remember Ed Chynoweth saying, 'Hey, Bob. What happened?' I told him, 'We weren't focused. We've got to change policies.'"

Canada finished at 2-3-2 and in sixth place. Lindros led them in scoring with two goals and eight assists. But in his short time at the helm, Nicholson could see that the team had deviated from the spirit of the Program of Excellence. The theme was to build the best team. Not just gather the best players and slap Team Canada jerseys on their backs.

"We changed the policy in the Program of Excellence the next year, and the biggest change was that all players had to be at the [December] selection camp, or they couldn't play," Nicholson said. "We got it out to the NHL teams, which they didn't like it at all. But we stayed strong on it. That's where we said: Team wins before individuals."

So, the next year when Pearn was assembling the 1993 team for Gavle, the focus was squarely on character. Which was why he named Martin Lapointe as his captain.

"We had Chris Pronger on defence, we had Paul Kariya, we had Rob Niedermayer. A ton of character people," Pearn said. "Whether you're talking about your elite player or your thirteenth forward, one of the things we looked at first and foremost was character. If you felt like your character was deep enough, then maybe you could put up with [a top six forward] who wasn't quite as deep in that area."

That year, Pearn and his staff faced a decision that was similar to, but different from, the one Habscheid would face a decade later with Tootoo.

"The guy we had to build character around was Alexandre Daigle. He was a superstar in Quebec and would end up going first overall in the [1993 NHL] draft," Pearn said. "Now, in hindsight, one of the things that has reinforced my evaluation of players over the years—and I've said it out loud many times—is how can anyone be picking Alexandre Daigle ahead of Pronger or Kariya? How can that happen?

"But it did, and I still consider that to be one of the best coaching jobs I did at that World Juniors. I played Daigle enough to make him look good, but not enough to have him hurt us."

It started in a crucial game against the hosts. Canada and Sweden would finish tied atop the tournament at 6–1, but they met in their second game. Though it was early in the tournament, it still had a gold medal feeling to it, and history tells us that would be an accurate read.

"Daigle took a penalty in that key game against Sweden. It gave me an opportunity to sit him for the rest of the game, which was big because he had a lot of defensive deficiencies," Pearn explained. "We were playing Russia the next game, and I sat him for the first half of that game, too. We wound up beating Russia 9–1, and I think he had two or three points once I started playing him.

"I looked like a genius: I'd disciplined him, so from a players' standpoint they're thinking, 'It doesn't matter who you are, he's willing to sit you.' And the flip side of it was, it motivated him enough that he came out flying. But he came out flying in a game we already had control of, leading four or five to one."

At the end of the day, when you sign on to coach a Team Canada, it becomes about taking the various different expectations—of players, of fans of Hockey Canada, of the junior operators who hand over their players—and somehow channeling them in the right direction.

Hunter's 2019 team didn't get the result they wanted, losing to the eventual gold medalists Finland in overtime of the quarterfinal. But his approach was thorough, even if his team came up a few goals short.

"Humility and compassion," Hunter explained. "You show [the players] how good the other teams are. Make them respect the other teams, and know that we're not going to do anything unless we check all the boxes.

"We have all our boxes—Canada's keys to success—and the one on the bottom is skill. Special teams. Work. Preparation. Team building. Our skill is the [lowest box]. We don't get there unless we have all these other boxes checked off first. You have to respect your opponent. The moment you don't, that's when it goes downhill."

Hunter's words echoed what we always knew: Canada would always have enough skill to compete internationally. We needed something more to put us over the top. We needed, as Costello predicted, an established Program of Excellence, one that drew on the strength of the teams that had come before it, like the one back in 1988 Moscow that had had the confidence to look the Soviets in the eye and refuse to blink.

CHAPTER 5

The TSN Deal

"I can't think of any challenges. It was all opportunity."

—RICK BRACE

Phil King was the business guy at TSN in 1989, and business was about to get good.

The Sports Network was just five years old, trudging along as a "premium subscription service." That meant the network was reliant on individual Canadian households to pony up roughly ten dollars per month to receive the channel, with the cable providers keeping roughly half of that. Dollars were tight and ratings were meagre, leaving TSN with two fairly obvious issues: It needed more sports properties, but it needed more money so it could buy those properties.

The ten-dollar-per-month fee pretty much ensured that TSN would never get past about a million subscribers. It became a glass ceiling on ratings. And of course, ratings dictate how much a network can charge for advertising, so the network's rate book had a hard cap on it as well.

That left TSN in a tough spot. Something had to change.

"You have to remember," King said, "TSN was created because of the Blue Jays. We were owned by Labatt's, which owned the Blue Jays, and they created TSN because they had so many of these damned ball games they couldn't get on TV. Back then, CBC would do a game a week. CTV would do a game a week. And that was it. There were four or five games each week where nobody saw the Blue Jays play. That's why it was created—by Gordon Craig, for Labatt's. And even then, we only did eighty games. The other games still weren't on TV, the late-night (West Coast) games, the getaway day [Thursday] games . . ."

Craig had come over in 1984 from the well-established CBC Sports to help found Canada's only all-sports network, and he quickly forged an alliance with a fledgling American network called ESPN. That gave TSN a steady diet of NFL, NASCAR, some PGA, and some tennis. Their portfolio of Canadian sports, however, was lacking.

By 1989, TSN really didn't have any championships outside of some low-rated Canadian university finals. They had Blue Jays games, but no Major League Baseball playoffs. They carried some CFL games, but no playoffs or Grey Cup. No finals of majors in tennis or golf, as they do today. In those early days, TSN would set the table, but Canadians would still have to go elsewhere—to the CBC, CTV, ABC, CBS, or NBC—to find the main course.

How does the cliché go? You don't know what you don't know? Canadians didn't realize how rinky-dink TSN was in those days, because we didn't have a clue what a real sports network was supposed to look like.

In the United States, ESPN was just a few years ahead in learning how voracious sports television consumers could be. They slowly found their niche by showing multiple college football games each weekend, where the traditional networks like CBS and NBC had given their viewers only one, often regional, game. As ESPN made some money and gained some respect, they began to challenge the major U.S. networks for properties like Major League Baseball and the National Hockey League, among others.

Up north, TSN's big break arrived just after its fifth birthday. King recalls it like one recalls the birth of their first child—as a gift from the gods. Or, rather, from the Canadian Radio-Television and Telecommunications Commission—the CRTC—a governmental body that, frankly, often acts as if it has some godly powers, overseeing all things radio and TV in Canada.

During my years in the Canadian media industry, a call or letter from the CRTC was unilaterally met with a nervous twitch from a radio or television executive. Truly, this particular arm of the government has well represented that old sarcastic axiom, "We're from the government. We're here to help."

This time, however, the news was good.

"On August 31, 1989, TSN was in about a million homes, give or take," King said. "So, we were in no position to go out and outbid anybody for big things because we were relatively small. But what happened was the CRTC allowed TSN to move to basic cable. That got us into five or six million homes."

If you do the math, this change in delivery didn't affect TSN's bottom line much. So, why was that such a big moment for The Sports Network?

"Well," said King, "all of the sudden the ratings went up—guess what?—five, six times. And so did the ad revenue."

There was no Sportsnet back then. The CBC was at the height of its privileged, government-funded existence, and CTV was barely a player on the sports scene.

TSN was the only dedicated sports game in town, and as a result, its ad rates skyrocketed. The challenge then became to find the right properties that could please all those viewers and attract new ones.

"I can't think of any challenges. It was all opportunity," said Rick Brace, TSN's director of programming at the time. "Overnight we went from having very little revenue, to broad distribution with a significant revenue stream."

Back in 1991, Brace was a young TV executive who had emerged from the production side of the business, where so many of the people who came to head the sports television world in Canada cut their teeth. Many of these people had found their way into the business because of their love for sports and their technical prowess, and then made the move from the TV truck to the executive suite in search of opportunity they had spotted along the way.

Like Brace, most of these "graduates" did a significant amount of their learning on the fly.

"We were killing it [financially] back then," Brace recalled. "The margins were massive. It really gave a lot of us an opportunity to learn the business side [of television] in an environment when we had the market to ourselves and the money coming in over the gunnels—against a backdrop of very little cost."

Not far from TSN's Leslie Street offices in Toronto, a couple of young guys were getting their start in the hockey production business as well. Their names were Paul Romanuk and Scott Moore.

Romanuk was a young TSN anchor who had broken into the business calling junior hockey on the radio, but had thus far been unsuccessful in finding his way into television play-by-play. Necessity being the mother of invention, Romanuk came up with the idea of a coast-to-coast CHL game, which of course he would call. So he brought in Moore, his old buddy from Ryerson University, as the production guy, and they sold their idea to TSN and the CHL in 1990: CHL Sunday Night, a national Major Junior game of the week.

This was yet another one of those TV ideas concocted by a couple of guys who were more interested in the opportunity than the income. There was no real money in junior hockey, but simply by watching TSN's lineup, they could see the network was content-starved. And if they could get a CHL Game of the Week off the ground, who knew what it might turn into?

"Right about then, the 'rights' to the World Junior Championship had come up," Romanuk said. "And I use the term 'rights' loosely, because nobody really paid much attention to it, unless it was in Canada. It wasn't a big sports property at all."

In the background, CAHA head Murray Costello, Rick Brace, and Bill Hay, who headed an organization called Hockey Canada that would later merge with the CAHA, were having conversations about the World Junior Championship. Under Costello, the CAHA had clearly enhanced the WJC product, and with the Program of Excellence now up and running, they could rightfully predict continued success as far as a hockey man's eye could see.

But the operative word in that last sentence is the final one: "see." The tournament was still mostly a well-guarded secret, a mighty Canadian maple that fell in the forest every Christmas. The CBC wasn't helping that, and it wasn't about the quality of its broadcasting. It was the CBC's commitment that left everybody wanting.

"All they'd say is," Costello said, "that they'd do the gold medal game—*if* Canada was in it. Other than that, they wouldn't even commit to televising the gold medal game."

In the early nineties, the CBC was simply too important to make a commitment on something at the level of the World Juniors. It was easy to sit on that high horse in those days, with government funding rolling in and virtually no competition on the Canadian sports television scene. The CBC owned *Hockey Night in Canada*, always carried the Olympics, and had the CFL after Labour Day, when the country returned from the lake and started to really pay attention.

The Canadians sports television landscape was their world, and every once in a while they'd let a CTV or TSN live in it for a while.

As Costello recalls it, the CBC executives made him and the CAHA feel as if they should consider themselves lucky that the CBC would grant the CAHA the opportunity to earn one game on mighty Mothercorp. As if the CBC was giving to charity—the irony being that no one got more free government funding than the network itself.

After the 1990 WJC, Costello finally told the CBC that he wasn't going to sign up for another year, that he'd look around instead. He had nothing to lose.

"I'll always remember the guy at CBC saying to me: 'You wouldn't dare take this product from the national broadcaster,'" Costello said. "I said, 'Oh, yeah?' He kind of talked as though he was in a position of strength. He felt he had the leverage to do it under his terms.

"Of course, the timing of TSN being where it was worked out perfectly for us."

By 1990, TSN had some money, and the ability to make much, much more with their situation vis-à-vis their advertising revenues. At the same time, the CRTC had these rules about Canadian content—called Can Con—which stipulated that TSN had to spend a certain percentage of their revenues on Canadian shows. Or in this case, Canadian sports.

The moment they could afford it, TSN had bought as much NHL hockey as it could, but in those days the regional packages worked differently from the way they do today, and the national games just weren't for sale, as they were all wrapped up by *Hockey Night in Canada*.

"Nothing but airtime, Monday to Friday, all winter long," King said. "So here you had a network with plenty of airtime. It's a network on the rise, it has money—money that it is required to spend [on Canadian content by the CRTC]—and now you had a partner in Hockey Canada that was saying, 'I want to grow, but not just Olympic hockey.' They wanted to grow women's hockey, juniors, domestic championships.

"So it was perfect. The right time, the right place for both organizations."

Dave Branch, the head of the OHL, had forged a relationship with Romanuk and Moore from their time doing the CHL Game of the Week, and he went to bat for them. "These guys have been really good to us," Branch told Costello, on behalf of all Canadian Hockey League junior operators. "We're the number-one providers of players to this tournament, and we'd really like them to be involved."

The people at the CBC, by all accounts, shrugged their shoulders.

"I can still vividly remember the day we signed the deal," said Brace. "There was Bill Hay, Jim Thompson [a founding partner of TSN], Murray Costello, myself, in Jim's office in Toronto.

"Bill was very bullish on getting the deal done. But Murray, his hands were shaking. He was really kind of, not sure."

This is where, almost thirty years later, memories don't always concur. Costello recalls being somewhat open to fleeing the cumbersome grasp of the CBC, but Brace remembers Costello being nervous about moving to this upstart TSN, basically trading a bird in hand for two in the bush.

"Murray, in particular, was really worried about taking it off the CBC, which had broad distribution but did a minimal amount of games," Brace said. "He loved the exposure, and leveraged us [at TSN] into doing all of the Canadian games. Which eventually grew into doing every game."

You can't blame Costelllo. This was his baby. The WJC was a property he had nurtured since birth, one that clearly had become the CAHA's most important asset. He knew before anyone else that the U-20 team would be the economic driver that would support the U-18 and U-16 teams, women's hockey, and anything else the CAHA was doing—kind of the way the Oklahoma Sooners football team funds many of the other University of Oklahoma teams, as well as pouring money into the academic coffers.

Costello had arranged the deal with the late TSN cofounder Jim Thompson, who would go on to become the CEO of the Canadian Olympic Committee before dying in 2002. Thompson's love of amateur sport in Canada was well known, and looking back, Costello remembered a negotiation that was both fair and gentle.

When they sat down at TSN's Toronto offices to talk about the property, Thompson said to Costello, "Look, let's forget about money for a minute, and just look at it like this: What are your needs? And I'll tell you what our needs are, because we're a cable company that's just starting up and we want to get into sports in a serious way. We need product."

"That's exactly what we've got," Costello replied. "And we need exposure for those events if they're going to be successful."

"We figured out our needs, and then we came back around and figured out the money later. It went exactly the way Jimmy said it would," said Costello, who got TSN to do something that the CBC would never do: commit to airing every Canadian game in the upcoming 1991 World Juniors in Saskatchewan. "Once that hit, we were away to the races."

The tournament coverage would eventually evolve to the point where TSN aired every game, be it Switzerland versus Denmark, or Kazhakstan versus Slovakia. That evolution was not a quick one, however.

"We used to do one semifinal." Phil King recalled. "We were terrified of doing a game that Canada wasn't in. Terrified! 'Oh, my gosh, who's going to watch Russia versus the United States in a semifinal? Billiards will do better.'

"And to be honest? In the first couple of years, billiards probably did do better."

The original contract was a five-year deal and was worth so little that nobody can really remember the actual number. It stated all the responsibilities of TSN, which included airing the Men's World Championships in May, and a certain number of games from things like the Women's Worlds and the Canadian Midget Championships. To this day TSN still airs events like the World Junior A Challenge, a loss leader that makes it to air only because it allows the network to also have blanket coverage of the WJC.

"The deal wasn't worth much back then. Might have been a hundred grand. Laughably low," said King, the TSN accountant at the time. "I can remember the World Hockey Championship being worth fifty grand a year, and going up five grand each year. It seemed like a lot back then. Now? I think that pays for about ten minutes of an Oilers game."

"It was more about the product being on air than the money," Costello said. "There was some money, but in addition to being on air, TSN really promoted it ahead of time. 'Watch for this tournament. You're going to see the future stars before they become stars.'"

Said Brace: "It wasn't about money. It was about exposure."

So TSN and the CAHA were wed. The honeymoon was set for Boxing Day in Saskatoon.

The temperature in Saskatoon, Saskatchewan, on Christmas Day 1990 was minus 32.5 degrees Celsius.

Cold?

"I have never experienced it that cold," said American Doug Weight, who would lead the 1991 tournament in scoring. "I remember the walk from the bus to the rink in Humboldt, where we played Sweden. What a great place to experience a World Juniors. One of my best hockey memories for sure."

On Boxing Day, Jim Hughson was up in the booth at the two-year-old SaskPlace press box, the trusty colourman Gary Green by his side. Hughson was calling NHL and Blue Jays games for TSN in those early years, but purchasing the WJC property was such a big deal for TSN that they pulled in their NHL crew to do the games.

"I was right in lockstep with the people at TSN, thinking that this was a really good property to pick up," Hughson said. "I didn't think it had received the exposure it should be getting. I thought this was going to be a big deal."

He hoped Canada would do well so that a maturing TSN would profit and the tournament would grow to the next level.

Paul Romanuk, who would go on to call eleven World Juniors tournaments, was hosting the broadcasts with journalist Bob McKenzie, who to this day is the ultimate authority on the WJC.

The tournament was stocked with future NHLers: Weight and Keith Tkachuk on Team USA; Michael Nylander and Tommy Salo on Team Sweden; Slovaks Ziggy Pálffy, Jozef Stümpel, and Czech goalie Roman Čechmánek.

The Russians were absolutely stacked with talent, including Pavel

Bure, Slava Kozlov, Boris Mironov, Alexei Zhitnik, and Dmitri Yushkevich. Latvians Sandis Ozolinsh and Sergei Zholtok, plus Lithuanian Darius Kasparaitis, were all players from the Baltic States who were who still playing in the Russian system.

On so many fronts, it was as if the World Juniors were being held for the first time. The TSN crew arrived en masse, ready to give the World Juniors a television treatment like it had never seen before, and hoping—no, planning—to hit a home run on their first trip to the plate.

"There were so many things that had to come together," Romanuk began. "We started off with a bang, because the tournament was in Canada. So, right away we are in the right time zone. The stands are going to be full. . . . You know, a lot has changed since then, but nothing has changed. By and large—and I can say this having lived overseas—even now, there's one country that truly gives a damn about this tournament, and you and I are sitting in it right now. Interest has gone up marginally in Sweden and Finland. Everywhere else, no one really cares about it."

There was only one problem. It was still 1991. TSN hadn't had their hands on this thing for much more than five minutes.

"Not even many Canadians even cared about it," Romanuk admitted. "The next year [1992], it was in Fussen, Germany. And I can distinctly remember my wife telling me that friends would ask her where I was over Christmas. She'd say, 'He's doing this junior hockey tournament over in Europe.'

"It sounds laughable now," he said, "but back then people had no idea. People in the hockey world knew how good this tournament was, but most people aren't in the hockey world."

That year in Saskatchewan, Canada had one player who was a household name in Canada: Eric Lindros, who everyone knew would be the number-one pick at the upcoming 1991 NHL Entry Draft in June. Much of the CHL coverage on TSN the previous fall had revolved around Lindros and his Oshawa Generals. The rest of the Canadian roster was laden with such future NHLers as Scott Niedermayer, Mike Sillinger, Patrice Brisebois, Steven Rice, Pat Falloon, Scott Thornton, Kris Draper, Brad May, and a kid from Newfoundland named John Slaney. The goalies were Felix Potvin and Trevor Kidd, who would combine to play more than a thousand NHL games. So there was pedigree here, even if most Canadians weren't aware of it.

Canada opened with a tidy 6–0 win over the Swiss, who never got out of, well, neutral. Then Canada tied the Americans 4–4 and blasted Norway 10–1 in a game played in Regina. The other tournament games were spread out across hockey-mad Saskatchewan, played inside prairie rinks in towns like Rosetown, Prince Albert, Moose Jaw, Kindersley, and Yorkton.

The Canadians walked through Sweden (7–4) and Finland (5–1) and stood at 4-0-1 after five games. The Soviets, meanwhile, were tearing through the competition. They were 5–0, and it was becoming apparent that the January 4 meeting between Canada and the USSR would be the de facto gold medal game.

But in a plot that just kept taking unseen turns for TSN and the CAHA, Canada coughed up a 6–5 loss to the Czechoslovaks on January 2. The result seemed disastrous as it was unforeseen. The Russians had a game against Finland the next day in Regina, and a win would wrap up the gold medal for the vaunted CCCP. You couldn't find a member of the Team Canada delegation who would have put twenty dollars on the Finns, even if you gave them two goals.

For TSN, what looked like a ratings bonanza—Canada-Russia, for all the marbles, on a Friday night from coast to coast—was now in jeopardy. The Thursday game between the Finns and Russians in Regina was set to let the air out of this tournament, and with it, TSN's maiden voyage at the World Juniors.

But rather than close its eyes and pray, the network did what a proper news organization should be expected to do. They spent a little money to cover the tournament the way it deserved to be covered.

"Something brand new that, as it turned out, would prime the pump for that final, gold medal game," said Moore, who, because of his involvement with Romanuk and the CHL Game of the Week program, had been asked by TSN to produce the 1991 WJC. "TSN had a National Hockey League game on that night. But we sold them on taking a small production truck down to Regina to do highlights and updates into their NHL game. At some considerable expense, I might say, which at the time was unusual for TSN. The response was good, because to that time, there had never been any coverage of a non-Canadian game at the World Juniors."

Romanuk and McKenzie made the 250-kilometre drive south to the Agridome in Regina—home of the Regina Pats of the Western Hockey League—for the Soviet-Finland game, where they would collect highlights to be shown during breaks in the NHL game on TSN that night. The two would give reports during the intermissions, and as it turned out, the trip to Regina couldn't have been a better idea.

Finland came out guns blazing, and with around six minutes to play in the second period, they'd launched into a 4–0 lead. Up in Saskatoon, the Canadian players were like a Pee Wee team at a Christmas tournament, their doors wide open and TVs on as players wandered the hotel floor waiting for another update to be piped into the NHL game.

The Finns held the Canadians' hopes in their hands, and don't kid yourself: No one had any particular faith in players like Jere Lehtinen and Juha Ylönen (whose son Jesse Ylönen would represent Finland in the 2019 WJC) to pull off the upset and save some Canadian bacon. The Canadians, Costello, and TSN had all turned to religion, praying that the Suomi could somehow upset a USSR team that had for generations been a goal or two better than Finland, with which they shared a border.

Sure enough, less than two minutes after the 4–0 goal, the Soviets scored one of their own. Then, before the Finns could reach the salvation of the second intermission, Bure sniped to make it 4–2. While Canada had Lindros, who dominated in a Canadian way with size, strength, and skill, Russia had Bure, who is still referenced today as perhaps the only person comparable to Connor McDavid when it comes to pure foot speed.

Bure came out of the dressing room in the third period like a man possessed, scoring less than five minutes into the period. Four–three for Finland. Then Oleg Petrov, who a few months later would become a sixth-round draft pick of the Montreal Canadiens, tied the game at the 11:08 mark. Then Bure secured his hat trick goal for a 5–4 Russian lead. As Romanuk and McKenzie delivered the news into the NHL broadcast, the heart inside every one of those Canadian kids in that Saskatoon hotel sank.

But then, with just over two minutes to play, Russia was assessed a too-many-men-on-the-ice penalty. The Finns, who had an outside chance at a bronze medal, pulled their goalie, and for a moment, something that closely resembled hope filled the Canadian air.

With less than twenty seconds to play, a young winger named Jarkko Varvio sent a prayer at the Russian net—a looping backhand from the far hashmarks. It was the kind of play intended more to get a puck into the danger area in front of the net than to actually score.

But score Varvio did, somehow slipping a puck underneath the butterfly of Soviet replacement goalie Sergei Tkachenko at 19:45 of the third period. The game ended in a 5–5 tie. After the final buzzer sounded, the standings read: Russia 5-0-1; Canada 4-1-1. That meant a Canada win over Russia would earn them a gold medal—a Canada-Russia classic for all the marbles. It was TSN's reward for having committed so many resources to the property.

Hughson recalls the name of the Finnish hero who tied the game as if he were his firstborn son. "I praise him whenever I think of him," Hughson said with a laugh. "We had the game we thought we would have. It was so important for us, in the evolution of TSN and the deal they'd made with Hockey Canada. And goodness knows, now they've never looked back. . . . They can thank Jarkko Varvio for that."

From there, the good luck just kept flowing for TSN. The Canada-Russia game was on a Friday night, wisely scheduled one day ahead of *Hockey Night in Canada*. Everything came up gold that night for Canada and TSN.

"Not only was it the first time that we'd made the deal to put all these games on television, but that exposure put a lot of pressure on them," Hughson said. "I had dinner with [Canadian head coach] Dick Todd during the tournament, and I could tell he was feeling the pressure immensely. Canada was supposed to win, and for the first time everyone in hockey was watching—and watching every game. And they were in their own country, so they couldn't hide from anything."

"We were experimenting with putting a microphone on some of the parents, and we asked Bonnie Lindros to wear a mic. But she wouldn't," Moore said. "We sent the audio assistant up, and he said, 'Bonnie won't wear it.' So I said, 'Just ask the woman next to her.' She turned out to be John Slaney's mom [Helen]. Sometimes you just have to have horseshoes, eh?" Moore laughed.

After watching the damage that Bure had inflicted on the Finns in Regina, the first decision Canadian coach Dick Todd made was to assign Kris Draper to shadow Bure. Draper went to work on Bure, and the drama of a low-scoring, gold medal game played out in front of a sell-out crowd inside Saskatchewan Place. There had only been two previous World Juniors played in Canada since the formation of the Program of Excellence—Winnipeg had only hosted early tournament games in 1992, while Hamilton did not experience a de facto gold medal game like this one when Copps Coliseum hosted in 1986.

The tension inside the arena in Saskatoon was thick as fog as the teams traded goals, going deep into the third period in a 2–2 tie. Then, with just less than six minutes remaining and the puck behind the Soviet goal, the Russians fired a puck around the right-wing boards. Rather than hold position and wait to receive the pass, though, the Soviet winger flew the zone for some reason. Slaney, stationed at Canada's left point, gathered the puck and walked into a slapper that broke the tie with 5:13 to play.

"Greg Johnson won the face-off, and it ended up going behind the goal," Slaney recalled. "All I remember is the puck came up the [right-wing] boards toward me, and I remember this Russian guy taking off [into the neutral zone]. I didn't feel any pressure at the time to back off the line and follow him. I just kind of lay low, and when the puck did come to me the most important thing was, you've got to get pucks to the net quick. Get it to the net, and hopefully the goalie's not set.

"When I did shoot it, it ended up going right between his legs. It was a quick reaction play. You walk in, tee it up, and hopefully it goes in. I was lucky enough that it did."

Hughson's call was testimony to what had become of this little U-20 tournament in our country: "It's a goal that spans Canada!

Jason Marshall from Cranbrook, B.C., to John Slaney from St. John's, Newfoundland, and Canada leads by one!"

The final five minutes were a blur for Slaney, and the bunch of Canadian kids who had never played in an atmosphere quite like this one.

"The crowd was so excited. They stood the entire last four and a half minutes," Slaney said. "For us, as the home team, it was important. They were the seventh player on the ice. Who knows? Maybe that was a factor for the Russians also. They never got many chances at the end."

Canada made it through the last few minutes, hanging on to win its first-ever World Juniors on home soil in a thrilling hockey game watched by Canadians from coast to coast. You could count TSN as yet another entity that had "discovered" the WJC as a winning formula.

"Once the ratings came out for that game," Moore said, "TSN realized they had a gold mine on their hands. You know, it's not unlike what cable sports has done generally. By showing more of the tournament, you create more interest and overall bigger audiences."

The ratings came in at somewhere around a million viewers. TSN would not confirm the numbers, and anecdotally, while Moore remembers a seven-figure game, others, such as King and Romanuk, say they never got to the magical one million number in '91.

"There weren't a million people watching. Not even close," Romanuk said. "It would have been in the healthy hundred thousands. I would bet it was about half a million. It wasn't a big event. It just wasn't."

From an exposure perspective, everything changed with that 1991 tournament in Saskatoon. Suddenly, the tournament was truly a sensation from coast to coast, and, coupled with the fact that most every province had a tie to at least one player, newspapers across Canada had sent reporters not only to cover the tournament, but to report on the exploits of "their guy" on Team Canada.

It was also an early example of how the red maple leaf was a uniting force that brought viewers from across Canada together, as opposed to the blue Maple Leaf that *Hockey Night in Canada* foisted upon Canadians every Saturday night. The World Juniors team, TSN would discover, engaged every Canadian hockey fan—a demographic that could dwarf even the mighty Southern Ontario region.

From that point on, TSN never looked back. In its earliest days, the WJC may not have been a big event, but boy, has it become one. In 2014, TSN re-upped with Hockey Canada on a new ten-year deal. The numbers are undisclosed, but on the heels of a 2011 gold medal game that drew 6.7 million viewers, the deal is estimated to be worth as much as $20 million annually.

That 2011 tournament was the most-watched event ever on Canadian cable television. Not bad for a little specialty channel started by a couple of guys from the CBC, eh?

"Because it was hockey, we knew it would have resonance," said Brace, whose name is on that original contract from 1990. "And because it was held at Christmastime, people were off work. They might not watch, but at least they were available to watch."

Did anybody see the possibility of this much success? That Canadians would come to watch World Juniors hockey at Christmastime the way U.S. families watch football on American Thanksgiving?

"No way," Moore said. "They thought they could do better at it than CBC because they had more airtime. Lee Herberman, the producer the year before, told me that this was some of the best hockey out there. That the kids were wearing the maple leaf on their jersey for the first time. That they were also playing for contracts, trying to impress NHL teams, and that they played with unbelievable emotion and heart.

"CBC didn't want to invest in it, and TSN saw the opportunity. We proved its value in that first year in '91, and they just continued to grow it," Moore said. "I think TSN deserves much, if not most, of the credit for making it such a big success. Not only for Hockey Canada, but for the IIHF as well."

"It would probably be too bold to say we knew this would be the greatest thing since sliced bread," Brace said. "But we all knew we were on to something. It was so darned Canadian."

As the 1991 tournament closed, players flew back to their junior and college teams, and the TSN mobile TV trucks pulled out for their next assignment. Canada had its first gold medal on home soil and the World Juniors had set sail on becoming the valuable TV property it is today. Not only had TSN learned there was value in showing each of Canada's games at the WJC, but their dalliance with that Russia-Finland game planted a seed that would germinate into the intensive schedule we know today.

What lay ahead was a string of gold medals that would foster a sustained national identity for the program. One that would be, as Brace put it, "so darned Canadian."

CHAPTER 6

Building the Business

"I'd never seen that much money."

—MURRAY COSTELLO

Bob Nicholson was working for British Columbia's provincial hockey body, B.C. Amateur Hockey. He was a technical director, a young guy on his way up in the hockey world, and he'd been working on a special project. His boss was a guy named Dave Andrews, who would later be named president of the American Hockey League, a position he still holds at the time of this writing.

"Dave hired me in '79–'80, and we built a program called the B.C. Junior Olympic Program," Nicholson said. "It was for forty-six players under seventeen in B.C., to give them a better coaching experience. Our coaches were Clare Drake and Dave King—not from B.C., but we thought they were the best coaches."

Sound familiar?

"The next year, the CAHA started the Program of Excellence."

It seemed preordained that Nicholson and Hockey Canada would intersect when Nicholson arrived at the CAHA offices in Toronto for the 1989–90 season—a business-minded amateur hockey man, and a Canadian Amateur Hockey Association that was just starting to get its head around the money side of things.

Upon Nicholson's arrival, the bid process for hosting the 1991 World Juniors was already under way. Nicholson was watching and learning as a committee made up of CAHA president Murray Costello, the legendary former Canadiens GM Sam Pollock, and CHL head Ed Chynoweth began the identification process of where they would place the 1991 WJC.

Nicholson would eventually become president of Canada's hockey body, and he would take them down some financial roads the CAHA never thought it would travel. But for now, Murray Costello was still in charge, and he flew his three-man group into Saskatoon late in 1989 for a look-see.

"We were met at the airport by one of the members of the host committee. Not the head of the committee, but one of his committee members," recounts Costello. "We get in a limo, and we're driving downtown when he says, 'Would it be all right if we made one short stop before we go to our meetings?' We said, 'Absolutely.'"

Saskatoon was a small place, and when you were coming in from Toronto or Ottawa, it seemed even smaller. Like the porcupine who fluffs his quills to make himself look bigger when challenged, the folks in Saskatoon had to do something loud and proud to make the most of this crucial first impression.

The limousine stopped at a downtown bank. A big bank, on a major intersection downtown.

"He took us right inside, walked us through the bank, and they opened the swinging doors. We walked through, into a back room, and inside that room were two pallets—you know, the kind they'd deliver beer on—and they were stacked with wrapped bills. Live currency. Mostly fifties, as I recall. They were piled up about five feet tall and filled two pallets."

The move had "Wild" Bill Hunter's fingerprints all over it. He was an old Western Canadian operator with Saskatoon roots who had pioneered the World Hockey Association, and who would later come *this close* to bringing the NHL's St. Louis Blues to Saskatoon in 1983. Hunter never met a publicity stunt he didn't like, and even though he wasn't part of the Saskatoon group, this huge pile of cash was vintage Wild Bill.

"They said, 'Gentlemen, that's one million dollars. If you bring the World Juniors [to Saskatoon] that is what you'll get,'" Costello recited. "I have to say, we were a bit impressed. We had not been dealing at those levels up to that point, and frankly, we'd wanted to be in the West that year. It looked like a good spot anyhow, and this certainly didn't hurt their cause."

Saskatoon backed up that big-money offer, hosting a legendary tournament. In the history of the WJC, 1991 would mark a crucial intersection of that bold Saskatoon host committee, the arrival of broadcaster TSN, and the CAHA's inkling that it was time to come out West. That was the year that the CAHA realized not only that the WJC could support all of the other levels of hockey within the Canadian amateur system, but that the financial risk could be more than just shared with the local host committee. It could largely be borne by the locals.

That day in the Saskatoon bank vault marked the end of cooperative efforts by host committees that saved money—through scads of volunteers, free rental cars, discounted room rates—in a system where no real money changed hands. "This was the first time anyone ever said, we'll take our chances, and regardless of what happens, this is what you'll leave with," Costello said.

That tournament was a turning point in many ways: Canada would win on the dramatic John Slaney goal, Canadian fans could watch all the games on TV, and the financial growth raised a bar that just keeps getting higher today.

"We were moving into an area that we never had really anticipated," Costello said. "We really owe a debt to Saskatoon."

Nicholson arrived at that Saskatoon World Juniors in 1991 as not much more than an interested observer. A million dollars seemed like a lot of money to the CAHA back in those days, and even though Nicholson hadn't had a lot to do with anything to that point, he would be the person who would take that $1 million and make it look like small potatoes down the road.

"Before it had been about just putting the best team together and trying to win the tournament," Nicholson said. "That was the start of, 'Hey, the World Juniors? There could be something here financially for us.'"

In Nicholson's twenty-six years with the CAHA, and then Hockey Canada, he would juggle responsibilities for both the on-ice and off-ice product, knowing that the success of one was necessary to fuel the success of the other. So in Nicholson's eyes, if the CAHA was going to be an entity that was now dealing in seven-figure bottom lines, it was time to start acting like one. That's when the shift occurred from the CAHA being about hockey, to being about hockey and profits.

Not coincidentally, it is also when they took the term "Amateur" out of their name.

"The big key here was the merger in 1994," Nicholson said. "Alan Eagleson was on his way out, and Sam Pollock was as well. It was Bill Hay from Hockey Canada and Murray Costello, president of the Canadian Amateur Hockey Association, who did the merger."

An entity known as Hockey Canada existed back then, and Eagleson was involved, along with Hay, whose father, Charlie Hay, was the quiet driving force behind the 1972 Canada-Russia Summit Series. Back in the seventies and eighties, the original Hockey Canada was an organization that staged pro events with NHL players, like the Canada Cup. It was also responsible for what was then a full-time Canadian National Team that operated out of Calgary, which represented Canada at the Olympic Games and major international tournaments—before the days when NHLers stocked many of those rosters. The odd time that an NHL player was in a contract dispute or found himself between jobs, he would join the national team for a while, as a way to both keep his skills sharp and have a bargaining mechanism against his NHL team.

As the CAHA matured into an organization that could command million-dollar deposits for a World Juniors, it became clear they were ready to handle the senior men's team, and any other events that needed organizing—even those including NHL players. Hay and Costello got together and merged the two entities, which meant an end to the "three sticks" logo that represented the Program of Excellence's three primary levels of focus: U-18, U-20, and the Olympic team.

"The biggest thing we did was, we went to one logo," Nicholson said. "We came up with the Hockey Canada logo." In came the crest we know today, with the red and black maple leaf, divided into halves by an oncoming, right-shot skater, striding off the centre of the jersey.

That logo debuted at the 1995 WJC hosted by Red Deer, with

Team Canada playing a single game at both the Calgary Saddledome and the Coliseum in Edmonton—the equivalent of the tournament putting its toe in the water when it came to holding games in NHL arenas. Those buildings would get two more games each featuring non-Canadian matchups, while the rest of the tournament took place in Red Deer and a bunch of Central Alberta towns such as Stettler, Innisfail, Wetaskiwin, Lacombe, and Ponoka.

"We did it where each small town adopted a team, and the kids would carry the players' bags. The players thought it was really cool," Nicholson said. "We played a Canada game in Edmonton and a Canada game in Calgary, and both were unreal games with huge ticket sales, and Red Deer packed all of their games. It really started to grow from there."

During the nineties, the Olympic Games would come to include a women's tournament, and the men's tournament would be forever transformed when the National Hockey League allowed its players to go to Nagano in 1998. Now the new Hockey Canada truly managed all levels of hockey in Canada, and really, it wasn't far off the Program of Excellence's original mandate that a player who was identified at sixteen years old would progress through to U-18s, through the U-20 program, and—back in those days—be prepared to join the national team program. Now it included women's hockey, too.

Still, the national team program had changed. It wasn't Dave King coaching a bunch of Canadian cast-offs in the Izvestia Cup or the Swedish Games anymore. It was guys like Jarome Iginla, Sidney Crosby, and Ryan Getzlaf wearing the Hockey Canada jersey, making memories in Olympic tournaments that have established themselves in Canadian hockey lore.

And, of course, that led Canadians to buy a lot of stuff along the way.

As it turned out, the '98 Olympics are recalled by Nicholson and most Canadians as "a *huge* disappointment." The men's team finished fourth, and Canada's women lost the gold medal game 3–1 to the United States.

The women's loss wasn't as alarming, because in the women's game it was—and often still is—preordained that the vastly superior programs of Canada and the U.S.A. would meet in the final. They did just that, and Canada lost a close game to a worthy opponent.

The men, however, vastly underachieved. After going 3-0 at the group stage, they squeezed past Kazakhstan 4–1 in the quarterfinal and then famously lost to the Czechs in a semifinal shootout in which Wayne Gretzky was left on the bench and Czech goalie Dominik Hašek thwarted our chosen shooters. Then we lost the bronze medal game to Finland, a classic case of the "gold medal or bust" attitude that has taken over Canadian hockey at the international level.

"But there was a silver lining in the loss," Nicholson pointed out. "We had the [Molson Open Ice] Hockey Summit in '99. We made the biggest changes that had ever been done to the Canadian game, over the next four years.

"We had the women in the Olympics, the NHLers in the Olympics, and a World Juniors [that] just took off in Winnipeg in 1999. It took another leap, and post-'99 we hired Wayne Gretzky, so now we had Gretzky branded in our logo going into the World Juniors at Halifax [in '03]."

So, how does one define progress along this jagged road of ascension for Hockey Canada? Well, when the NHLers and Canadian women went to Nagano in '98, Hockey Canada sold $100,000 worth of jerseys.

"In 2010 in Vancouver, we sold thirty million dollars," Nicholson said.

That's quite a leap, and it didn't happen overnight. The process of merchandising had actually begun long before, when a fellow named

Bruce Newton worked as a marketing contractor to the CAHA at the first Canadian World Juniors, in Hamilton. His company provided game-day programs, board ads, and a level of merchandise that was, at best, antiquated compared to today.

Back in 1986, Newton's company would sell you a branded T-shirt, a sweatshirt, a ministick, maybe a puck. "Very basic stuff," he said. "I don't even think we had a jersey to sell back then."

If they did, it sported the old CAHA logo, which in itself wasn't very compelling. But remember, in 1986 you couldn't just walk into the local mall in Burlington and buy, say, a Los Angeles Lakers jersey the way you can today. It was a different time in merchandizing, and on top of that, Hockey Canada was still a minor league organization.

"There just wasn't going to be a company that was willing to stick its neck out on inventory," Newton explained of the early days. "And the CAHA wasn't in a financial position to stick its neck out either."

Nicholson recalls a story from 1992 in Fussen, Germany. "I remember calling Murray Costello from Germany and saying, 'Murray, we're watching freakin' videos on my bed here. Can we get another room?' And he said, 'Bob, we have no money. We couldn't get a meeting room.' That's where we were financially."

But, as the stature and popularity of the World Juniors grew, the new Hockey Canada figured out how to monetize that growth—both in jersey sales and within the television property.

"I think interest grew in the whole tournament when we went into the playoff format [in 1996]. Especially for TSN," Newton said. That year, the tournament abandoned the old round-robin format in favour of the sudden-death playoff round. "Once they could say, 'Canada is in the gold medal game,' a thirty-second spot on TSN just jumped through the roof."

You'd think the network had a lot to do with that, and they

no doubt made every attempt to influence the decision. But the reality was that the IIHF was in many ways a stodgy, old, European-based, boys club. They weren't about to bow to the TV networks the way leagues do today, and back then there wasn't enough money involved to sway the IIHF. The international hockey organization was, in fact, more interested in adding more teams than in changing their format for TV. The tournament had expanded, taking in Slovakia and adding the perennial doormat Ukraine as well. The two new teams, more than any pressure from the networks, were the reason for the tournament adopting the kind of sudden-death format that North Americans prefer. More importantly, that North American TV prefers.

"It helped push the business," Newton said. "But on merchandise, as much as the World Juniors heightened awareness, what really moved the business was when we developed our brand. The logo we have today."

Newton leafed through Gare Joyce's compendium, *Hockey Canada—Thirty Years of Going for Gold at the World Juniors*, in search of the first time the new logo was used, and which apparel company was building the Team Canada uniforms. He gave a play-by-play as he turned the pages.

"In Hamilton [in '86] we wore Cooper," he said. "In '88, the IIHF went to a single supplier jersey for all their championships, so that year we were actually wearing Adidas. Then we went back to Cooper the next year, and in 1990 it went to Tackla. In '94 we wore Reebok jerseys, but with Tackla pants! So '95 in Red Deer was the first year we had the Hockey Canada logo, but it was a Reebok jersey. In '96, that's when Nike bought Bauer. Nike divided up the countries, and while some countries were Nike brand, we were Bauer brand.

"It wasn't until Winnipeg in 1999 when everyone switched to Nike. And we're Nike through to today."

Hockey Canada's longstanding partnership with the world's largest athletic apparel sponsor is a symbol of how far the World Juniors has come, from the early years when they would buy their uniforms from down the street at Cooper Canada, to today, when they deal with the big boys in the sporting apparel industry. Along the way, of course, everyone has come to make some serious profits off of those jersey and merchandise sales.

When it comes to marketing, NHL jersey sales have a level of regional restrictions to them. For the most part, a fan in Vancouver isn't buying a Habs jersey, and an Oilers fan isn't spending money on Maple Leafs apparel. But Hockey Canada figured out early on that theirs was the only hockey logo that was loved equally across provincial lines from coast to coast.

"We play that up big-time," Newton admitted. "One of the real cool things is, I'll be at a game in London with the women's team, and I'll see a jersey that's ten years old, if not older. I saw in Vancouver [in 2019]—a lot of people wearing the 2010 Olympic jersey. It's amazing how much current and historical branding you see at a Team Canada game today.

"And," he noted, "I can pick out the counterfeit ones, too."

Through it all, whether we're talking merchandising, ticket sales, or television properties, the World Juniors has become Hockey Canada's mainstay, the "Steady Eddie" property that puts the jersey in front of millions of Canadians annually. At the senior levels, Canada won gold in men's and women's at the Salt Lake City Olympics in 2002. Then, just as the brand was at its apex, they had the 2010 Vancouver Olympics. It seemed as if things couldn't get any better for the brand: The World Juniors team had just completed a run of five gold medals in a row from 2005 to 2009, both the men and women won Olympic gold that year in Vancouver, and in 2006, the IIHF had decided to host every second World Juniors tournament in Canada.

"That brought sponsorship, and not just for World Juniors," Nicholson said. "[Current president and CEO] Scott Smith deserves a lot of credit here, because we didn't just get sponsors for the World Juniors, we had them take a bite of everything."

The 1999 Hockey Summit had produced several new initiatives, the Esso Medals of Honour being one. It provided Hockey Canada with some options for sponsors and a way to extract dollars by spreading out their involvement across different age groups and programs—think the Royal Bank Cup Junior A Championship and the Telus Cup for Midgets.

But as the business was growing, they could not forget it was the on-ice product that fuelled everything. If winning all these medals was helping business, then losing could take it in the opposite direction, right? It was, at its very roots, Costello and McDonald's Program of Excellence that had provided the foundations for all this good business.

Starting in 1993 in Gävle, Sweden, Canada would enter a stretch where it would medal in nineteen of the next twenty World Juniors. Through some trial and error, Hockey Canada was circling around the perfect formula: a superior program, a Christmastime tradition that was growing exponentially, and constant success that was a no-brainer for Canadian hockey fans to get behind.

It all meant dollars for the program. And the IIHF wanted a piece of the action.

Originally, back in the seventies, eighties, and nineties, Canada would host one out of every five tournaments. Then one out of four. Then every third year. By 2006, it became every other year. It made good financial sense—the profits from tournaments held in Canada far exceeded those reaped from anywhere else in the world.

The reasons for Canada hosting so much more than other countries are simple: The IIHF can charge Canadian host committees a hosting fee that far exceeds what Ostrava, Malmö, or Ufa could afford to pay. In turn, Canadians are charged ticket prices that far exceed what European (or American) fans are willing to pay, and they fill NHL-sized buildings, buying the requisite amounts of beer, food, and Hockey Canada/IIHF apparel.

Off-site, millions more Canadians watch the games when they are taking place in a time zone that is prime time in Canada, as opposed to 6:00 a.m. games coming out of Europe. Those extra viewers pump up TSN's ratings, which shoots their ad rates through the roof, which keeps the price rising every time a new contract is negotiated.

It was clear that Canada was the one country that had really fallen in love with the World Juniors. The cash simply flowed from there.

"Hockey is growing, rising now in Germany," said Franz Reindl, the president of the German hockey federation who was a cochair of the 2019 WJC in Vancouver and Victoria. "But having a junior world championship, it cannot compare to here in Canada. It is another level, it's another event."

"Easily the top ten attended events have been held in Canada," Newton points out. "And our tickets are significantly more expensive here than when it's hosted elsewhere."

The success peaked in 2012, when they rolled into Alberta just as Fort McMurray was producing oil that sold for over $100 per barrel. Albertans were flush with cash and living in a province that couldn't get enough of what Hockey Canada was selling.

"We had to have a lottery for the tickets that year," Newton said. "When it came time to sign up, it crashed our website."

The 2012 WJC in Alberta was the granddaddy of them all, economically speaking, for Hockey Canada. Two NHL buildings, a booming economy, and a Canadian team that had made it to ten consecutive gold medal games.

Like the oil boom, everything was through the roof at that WJC. They sold 495,000 tickets that year in Edmonton and Calgary, compared to 304,000 in B.C. in 2019. The take-home share of the 50/50 draw soared over $100,000 on several nights. Los Angeles Kings scout Mike Futa even got into the fun, when he won about $87,000 on a lucky 50/50 ticket at a game between Canada and the Czech Republic.

Off the ice, business was on a steady rise, with no real competition from the other hockey countries when it came to successfully hosting the WJC. On the ice, however, the other countries were not enamoured of losing to Canada so consistently. It was getting harder and harder to maintain the dominance that had been linked to Hockey Canada's program, and Nicholson knew that Canada's place at the top was one bad bounce away from being usurped.

"When we lost after five in a row [in '98]," Nicholson said, "you've got to remember the pressure. 'You've got to win six!' We were playing the Russians in a quarterfinal, and with twelve seconds to go Eric Brewer goes post-to-post and out. That goes in, and we're right back at 'er. It doesn't go in, we lose, there's such huge disappointment, and we get thwacked by Kazakhstan. We'd never been in that position, because before that it had always been a round-robin. And we lost."

Roberto Luongo was the backup goalie in Helsinki in 1998, playing behind Mathieu Garon. As the tournament got going, somehow that Team Canada just never found the mojo that the previous five had discovered.

"We all knew they'd won five in a row, and there was a little bit of pressure on our club," Luongo said. "Obviously we didn't get the job done. We didn't lack talent, but the thing I remember is, we just didn't come together as a team. At the end of the day that's what did us in."

They'd done all the pretournament team-building sessions and followed the Hockey Canada protocol.

"We did all that stuff," Luongo said. "Sometimes you just don't get the right mix of guys. Not that we had any bad guys on the team, but it wasn't the right combination. It just didn't happen for us. You could see on the ice, when we were playing. It was just a bunch of guys playing hockey together. Not the Canada we see almost every year."

Nicholson had seen the pressure building during that first-five-in-a-row run, like a balloon hooked up to an unmanned pump. So he and his team came up with a new strategy.

"We asked the players to give us a 'gold medal performance.' We tried to say, 'Hey, if you give us a gold medal performance and don't win gold, that's acceptable,'" Nicholson recalled. "But, the media didn't buy it. And the players in the room, they saw those gold medals going around Canadians' necks when they were twelve-year-old kids. When they're named to that team, that's where their head goes. To the gold medal."

That's not the only Hockey Canada plan that never grew legs, however. Years later, Hockey Canada granted the 2015 and 2017 tournaments to Montreal and Toronto, with the theory being they would flip-flop the Canadian Group and the medal round in each year. It didn't work, and there were lots of empty seats.

"We charged too much, and we should never have gone back-to-back," Nicholson said. "There was huge interest in both of those cities and we wanted them both to see medal rounds. One might have [succeeded], but when they learned there were two in three years, the prices got too high."

In 2019, Hockey Canada took the unprecedented step of "awarding" the WJC to Edmonton and Red Deer in 2021, eschewing the usual bid process. That's how confident Hockey Canada was in the Alberta market, their NHL-CHL venue formula, and Canadians' love for what the WJC has become.

Culturally, Costello had dreamed of something like this back in the 1980s. But never in his wildest dreams did he see the World Juniors becoming this entrenched in Canadian culture.

"We just wanted to win," Nicholson said of the early days. "Then you went, 'This is starting to become a Christmastime tradition!' Then it went from that to Canada's Super Bowl.

"The game became healthier when you could tie so many kids' dreams to it. The Olympics come every four years, but the World Juniors is every year. Hopefully that gets them on the ice to play the game of hockey."

And if they turn out to be elite, and catch the eye of the Program of Excellence, the evolution of the World Juniors has ensured there is plenty of money to take a Canadian kid around the world.

CHAPTER 7

The Best There Ever Was

"I look back on that team and the biggest compliment is that people say it was the best World Juniors team ever. To be a part of that as a player, it's a pretty big honour."

—DION PHANEUF

Birth years dictate success at the World Juniors as much as anything else. Sometimes, a particular birth year will give Canadian hockey an inordinate amount of talent, and other years, some lucky coach goes to a Hockey Canada summer camp and finds 30 percent more talent than the coach found twelve months before.

Other times, that birth year is so good that a bunch of U-20 eligibles are playing in the National Hockey League—and the World Juniors team is weaker for it.

The crop of players born in 1985 was truly special, stocked full of hockey newborns who would win gold medals at every level, from U-16 to the Olympic Games. They had names like Dion Phaneuf, Ryan Getzlaf, Shea Weber, Corey Perry, Andrew Ladd, Jeff Carter, and Mike Richards. Then, as they entered the final season of junior eligibility in 2004–05, the draft class's last season of amateur eligibility, they ran right into a National Hockey League lockout.

"Our whole draft class spent a lot of time with each other," remembered Phaneuf. "Coming out of the Western League with me, Webs, Getz, Ladder, Shawn Belle, you'd be doing things with these guys all the way up to the draft. And then we were playing against each other in the Western League a lot. You cross paths at different games: All-Star games, Canada-Russia Series. . . . By the time we got to Grand Forks we'd played a lot of hockey together."

The Team Canada that roamed the ice in Grand Forks, North Dakota, at the 2005 World Junior Championship was a freshly shorn group so stacked with talent that Czech coach Alois Hadamczik openly mused before his team's semifinal meeting with Canada, "It would be good if they let us play both of our goalies at once."

Twelve players returned from the year before, a paralyzing loss in Helsinki where Marc-Andre Fleury's clearing pass had banked into the net off the shoulder of Canadian defenceman Braydon Coburn during the gold medal game, gifting the Americans the tournament-winning goal. How many of those returnees would have been playing in the NHL had it not been for the season-long lockout? Who knows?

This much we can be sure of, however. Several would have had lengthier locks had it not been for coach Brent Sutter's edict when the team arrived in Grand Forks.

"I don't let guys on our team at home [the Red Deer Rebels] who have long hair," Sutter said with a shrug. "I don't let my own kids have long hair. And it's not a big deal to them, either. It's accepted."

Canada had not won a World Juniors gold medal in the past seven tournaments, and when it became clear that the lockout would not impinge on the roster for the 2005 World Juniors, well, it seemed a foregone conclusion that streak would be snapped. The last time Canada had fielded a WJC team in a lockout year was 1995, when the team went 7-0. Ryan Smyth, Ed Jovanovski, Eric Daze, Bryan McCabe, Wade Redden, Todd Harvey, Jeff O'Neill, Darcy Tucker—they had won gold going away in Red Deer that year, and this time around, in 2005, the names were even sexier.

A seventeen-year-old Sidney Crosby joined a bevy of nineteen-year-olds that included Patrice Bergeron, Brent Seabrook, Weber, Getzlaf, Carter, Richards, Phaneuf, Ladd, and Perry. It was, almost certainly, the best roster ever to be assembled for a World Juniors, from any country. History bears that out, with the names on that roster having gone on to win a combined seventeen Stanley Cups. But before any pucks were dropped for Team Canada that Christmas in North Dakota, some hair would hit the floor.

"I talked to Dion Phaneuf and Colin Fraser, and asked them: 'Does [Sutter] do this back in Red Deer?'" said Perry, whose hockey hair always flowed from underneath his London Knights helmet. "And they said, 'Yeah, everybody on the team has to have short hair.'"

Perry, who had suffered the unkindest cut of all as the last player trimmed from the 2004 Team Canada roster, lined up for his buzz cut in North Dakota with some measure of glee, much preferring to be coiffed on Team Canada, rather than long-haired in London.

"He just wants us to look like professionals and act like professionals," Perry said of Sutter. "I had to shrink the helmet a little bit, but it doesn't matter. We're so ecstatic to be on this team, we'd do anything to be on it."

Richards and Bergeron were also directed toward the barber's pole, as was defenceman Danny Syvret, who played with Perry in London. The Knights had just come off a record thirty-one-game unbeaten streak in the Ontario Hockey League, and nobody on head coach Dale Hunter's squad wanted to jinx the winning skein by changing anything—even the length of their hair.

For Sutter, that was all the more reason for conformity.

"Those kids from London," he said, "they get into those rituals where they're on a streak and don't want to change anything. But my view is that once you get here, it starts over. I wanted a fresh start, everybody to be on the same page, whether it's on the ice or off the ice. It's about trying to create a team, and bond as a team, as quick as possible."

"There were," Syvret said, "four guys that had to go—but almost the whole team went along, just to stay together. Probably twelve or fourteen of us. We weren't in a position to argue with him [Sutter], so I think in an hour we all had our hair cut. It didn't bother me. I was so high on making the team, I didn't care what my hair was gonna look like. When you haven't won a gold medal in eight years or whatever it is, you need to make sure you're all on the same page."

Thirteen years later, Weber laughs at the memory. "We had a rule in Kelowna," he said. "If you had a haircut coupon in your stall, it was time to get a haircut. [Team owner] Bruce Hamilton's rules."

As is the way of the hockey player, the Canadian kids found their way through with humour.

"The guys have been giving it to Corey," Syvret said with a laugh. "With his hair so short, they said they didn't realize what a small head he has."

They kid because they love. And as a veteran coach, Sutter knew that when he heard his players having some lighthearted fun at the expense of Perry, his team was coming together.

You see, this wasn't like most World Juniors teams, where it becomes a race to install a system, define roles, and teach new terminology before Game 1. Of course, all those things had to occur, but with a team that was loaded with this unprecedented level of talent, Sutter wisely used scenarios that would bring the players closer together, creating bonds that would result in nobody stepping outside of the confines of what Sutter defined as "team."

"There were a lot of returning guys on that team, and they'd lost a tough one the year before." said goalie Jeff Glass. "They'd gone seven years without winning the gold, and Brent Sutter had everybody dialed in. When he spoke, everyone listened, and we were all pulling the rope in the same direction. But as good as that team was, we hadn't won anything yet. There was zero sense of complacency."

"He talked about how most guys on this team were first-line or star players on their junior team," Weber said. "We were going to need guys who are used to scoring big goals to play a third-, fourth-line role. Guys to penalty kill who are used to playing powerplay. Guys are going to have to sacrifice what they're used to doing for the good of the team."

At the summer camp, Red Deer Rebels teammates Phaneuf and Colin Fraser had squared off in one of the first scrimmages.

"Me and Sid would always battle with each other," Phaneuf recalled. "I hit Sid in one of the scrimmages, and Colin Fraser came at me and we actually fought. We were teammates in Red Deer and close friends, and I remember seeing Fraz in the back hallway after the game. We were joking about it after, but we were competitive guys. We pushed each other."

Fraser was protecting a Canadian teammate in Crosby ahead of a WHL teammate in Phaneuf.

"That's the kind of team it was," Sutter said with a shrug. He knew that fight would bring Phaneuf and Fraser closer as teammates both for Red Deer *and* for Canada, a perverse bit of hockey culture that some find difficult to understand.

No, this wouldn't simply be an All-Star cruise through the World Juniors where nobody hit anyone, and everyone played with a smile on his face. Sutter would seek out complacency in every corner of the dressing room and eradicate it, instincts learned from his primary coaching influences serving as his sniffer dogs. Where Brent Sutter coaches, by extension so, too, does the legendary Al Arbour, Sutter's coach with the New York Islanders, as well as Mike Keenan, his brother Darryl Sutter, and the old coach from his junior days with the Lethbridge Broncos, John Chapman.

Sutter's mantra?

"Just keep them sharp, in everything we did," he said. "Making sure we weren't late for one meeting. Making sure we did everything together as a group. Making sure that we were eating right. Everything those kids did, they did together.

"You knew they were great players, it was just the details. Making sure we were sharp, every day. And for three and a half weeks, we were. We were a driven group, and we never took our foot off the pedal."

Sidney Crosby—Patrice Bergeron—Corey Perry

Andrew Ladd—Ryan Getzlaf—Jeff Carter

Nigel Dawes—Mike Richards—Anthony Stewart

Clarke MacArthur—Stephen Dixon—Colin Fraser

(Jeremy Colliton)

Dion Phaneuf—Shea Weber
Braydon Coburn—Brent Seabrook
Danny Syvret—Shaun Belle
(Cam Barker)

Jeff Glass
(Rejean Beauchemin)

Nice lineup, eh?

Crosby was just seventeen, and he might have been the team's best player. Bergeron, who had played seventy-one games for the Boston Bruins the previous season, had been farmed to AHL Providence during the lockout because he was young enough for the assignment under the Collective Bargaining Agreement. But Bergeron knew the AHL was the wrong place for him that Christmas.

"It was important for me to go [to North Dakota]," said Bergeron, now a thousand-game NHLer, an annual Selke Trophy candidate, and one of the truly elite players in the world. "I asked to go if I could, and obviously Boston was nice enough to release me. I think I missed twelve games [in Providence] just for that tournament. It was a big commitment for Boston to do, but I felt it was something I was watching on TV growing up and every time around Christmastime I was watching the Juniors and I wanted to be a part of it. . . . I also had an idea that we were going to be pretty good. So you want to be a part of a winning team like that. There were some pretty special players and special guys that turned out to have some amazing careers. We became friends and it was a pretty close group for a two-week tournament."

Sutter had watched Bergeron take Crosby under his wing right from the beginning of the summer camp, and he made them roommates when the team reconvened in December. "They were the perfect match. You just knew there was chemistry between them," Sutter said. "You knew that both would be great players, and now you look back at these two kids, you watch them at international competitions today? They play together."

Clearly the coaching staff—including assistants Peter Deboer, Jim Hulton, Rob Cookson, and goalie coach Ian Clark—knew that the top end of its lineup would, er, suffice. But building a team, as Canadians had learned, entailed more than simply picking the top twenty-two scorers in the league and handing them a uniform.

Canadian hockey people have always fixated on roles, chemistry, and team building. When we win, there is ample credit for getting the "formula" right. But when Rob Zamuner makes the 2008 Olympic team ahead of Mark Messier, or when Canada goes to a shootout and leaves Wayne Gretzky on the bench—and we finish fourth in Nagano—oh, boy, we can sling the blame with the best of them.

So as they constructed that team for North Dakota, from a pool of talent that was deeper than any before or after because of the lockout, Hockey Canada recalled its commitment to building a true *team*. Four lines with the right chemistry of penalty killers, grinders, goal scorers, and powerplay guys. Three defensive pairings with the right mix of skill and defensive prowess.

"It was certainly an elite group. It was just about what we would fit around them, the chemistry," Sutter said. "There were players like Ryan Stone, a top scorer in [WHL Brandon]. But we were looking for guys who brought the heavy work. The guys on the boards. Players who could win face-offs."

In goal, Sutter settled on Glass and Beauchemin, two goalies who had not even been invited to the summer camp. There, as it turned out, the goalies had merely been placeholders so Sutter could scout netminders during the first three months of the Juniors season. Sutter knew exactly what he wanted in his goalies, but before he could decide whom to take, he needed to see the first half of the CHL season unfold.

"We knew we would be a team that would give up less than twenty shots against a game, so we needed to have a goalie who came from a program that didn't give up a lot of shots. We obviously needed a really good goalie, but one who could keep himself in games mentally, and keep going," no matter how few touches he had.

Glass, who played for the Kootenay Ice, lost just eleven games that regular season, and allowed the fewest goals in the Western Hockey League. Beauchemin, out of Prince Albert, played one game for Canada and faced seven shots. He had a shutout.

"It was just finding the right fit," Sutter said. "Then, we became a team that gelled. When you have that many star players on your team, you have to park the egos, and let's everyone just bring it all the time. Our practices were outstanding, and it carried on through to the games."

Finally, Christmas Day arrived. And with that, the present that was Game 1 of the 2005 World Junior Championship for Canada, at the beautiful Ralph Engelstad Arena in Grand Forks, home of the University of North Dakota Fighting Sioux. First up, Slovakia.

What do you think happened?

"It was cold, I remember that," Ryan Getzlaf said of Grand Forks. "And the building, every game was like a home game for us. The building was rocking, and it was probably one of the best buildings I'd ever played in, at that point in my life."

Manitobans poured over the border and into North Dakota, making "the Ralph" a sea of red. And speaking of red, they undoubtedly saved this tournament from drowning in red ink, as support from south of the forty-ninth parallel was spotty at best. One thing the IIHF had learned: If they were going to hold a World Juniors in the U.S.A., it had better be a reasonably close drive from the Canadian border, like Grand Forks or Buffalo. Then the "Canadian effect" would apply, making tickets scarce and beer sales robust.

Canada opened with a 7–3 win over the Slovaks, a fairly sloppy effort considering that through the rest of the tournament, Team Canada would never again allow more than one goal against in a single game. They then walked through Sweden 8–1 and walloped the Germans 9–0.

As Canada worked through a flawless 4–0 preliminary round in Group B, the media around the team began to figure something out: Watching Canada practice was, to this point in the tournament, as intriguing as watching them play. Perhaps more so.

At a little rink called Gambucci Arena, media people leaned over the iron railings overlooking the ice surface below, drinking in a Canadian morning practice with speed that made you gasp, witnessing skills they could scarcely believe. After three games in four nights, this was perhaps the best hockey Team Canada had played.

"Their practices were as intense as any game they played," said then-TSN analyst Pierre McGuire. "Those were the days when Dion Phaneuf and Sidney Crosby, who were friends, would go after each other in practice like you wouldn't believe. It was tremendously intense."

At this practice, late in the preliminary round, the Canadians played three-on-three inside the blue-line, the nets pushed to the boards near the hashmarks. It made for tight quarters and demanded high-skill maneuvering, made more difficult by teammates standing just outside the blue-line awaiting their turn, poke-checking any puck carrier who ventured within reach.

The Hockey Hall of Fame columnist Cam Cole was my colleague at the *National Post* in 2005, as he had been at the *Edmonton Journal* before that. And when I say "colleague," what I really mean is "mentor." He was on par with Michael Farber atop the pecking order of daily Canadian sports columnists, and as such, he drew the assignment to travel to North Dakota for the *National Post* in 2005. Cole was at that Gambucci Arena as Canada practiced before their final preliminary round game against the Finns.

"All we could think, as we watched the frenetic pace, the precision passing, the size and speed and skill assembled on that surface, was: If this isn't the best Canadian Juniors team ever assembled, we'd love to see the team that would beat them," Cole filed to the *National Post* that day. "And one more thought: maybe the 35–4 collective margin by which they have beaten Finland, Switzerland [pretournament], and Slovakia, Sweden, and Germany is not because the opposition is so weak. Maybe these guys are really that good."

Crosby, who had played the year before in Finland in front of far fewer media eyes, was now making a first impression on scribes like Cole. Usually, the veteran sportswriter is met with a player who doesn't live up to the hype. Not this time, however.

"Six goals, he's got, in three tournament games—five of them on the powerplay, tying a tournament record—yet your eye is not drawn to him, the way it was to Bobby Orr or Mario Lemieux," Cole wrote. "You begin to understand, though, why Wayne Gretzky immediately saw the magic in him. What he has is Gretzky's kind of subtle sleight of hand."

Canada would throttle the Finns to close out a perfect preliminary round. They would get two days off while the quarterfinals were played, awaiting the winner of a game between David Krejči's Czechs and Tuukka Rask's Finns. The Czechs, on the strength of a 3–0 victory, would be fitted with the lamb costumes for their January 2 march to the slaughter against Canada.

The day before Canada's final preliminary round game, a wicked prairie snowstorm blew through the Dakotas, icing down vehicles and burying Grand Forks in a layer of snow so thick that, late in the opening period, organizers felt obliged to inform the crowd over the PA system that the Royal Canadian Mounted Police had closed Highway 75, stranding a few thousand Manitobans who had planned on heading home during the two days between Canada's games.

Those folks had not only saved the 2005 World Junior Championship from being a financial debacle, they had lent to the uniqueness of the event by making Canada the de facto home team, even on American soil. Now they'd stay a little longer and make another trip to the ATM—and to the liquor store, of course.

The things a hockey fan has to do for his or her country.

"It was almost like being at home," said Steve Getzlaf, Ryan's dad. "It was so close to Winnipeg. It didn't matter where you went, what part of town, you ran into Canadians."

With hotel rooms maxed out in Grand Forks and the surrounding area, organizers opened up the Alerus Convention Centre overnight so the Canadians would have a place to bed down and weather the storm. Of course, for Canadians decked out in Hockey Canada garb and in a holiday hockey mood, it just became a reason to have more fun.

"I bet most of those people wouldn't even think twice about it," said Dawes, a Winnipeg native who has settled in with Astana Barys of the KHL, where he annually challenges for the league lead in goals and points. "It's an adventure for them to drive through that snow, another war story they can tell their grandkids someday."

Canada had not yet met the Czechs, their semifinal opponent, as the Czechs had advanced from Group A with Russia and the United States. Nor had Canada seen firsthand the work of goalie Marek Schwarz, who played for the Vancouver Giants. Sutter knew Schwarz from the Western League, but the game turned out to be a fine example of how a team can get caught in a sudden-death situation—especially a team that had not faced any adversity yet in the tournament—and receive a scare.

The Czechs were able to hang around, which was more than anyone else had done to that point against Canada. But to take their dream of an upset and make it a reality, they would need for Canada to blow some oxygen into the embers of Czech belief. To make a mistake or take a bad penalty. Cough up a puck that ended up behind Jeff Glass—anything.

This was the game Sutter had prepared his charges for. They would add no fuel to the Czech fire while scoring three goals of their own. Then Canada would watch as the clock ran out in a 3–1 game that was as stern a test as that group of Czech juniors could ever have hoped to administer to the future superstars from Canada.

As it turned out, it was a test. But it was a test the Canadians had been waiting for, and one they had absolutely no doubt they would pass.

"Our hardest game was that semifinal against the Czechs," Glass confirmed. "We got up by a couple of goals, and we locked it down. We weren't going to lose, and whether the score was going to be 6–1 or 2–1, we were going to win that game. Everyone really bought into what Brent was selling."

If hockey is a game of mistakes, well, Canada simply didn't make any in that semifinal, outshooting the Czechs 26–4 through the first forty minutes, and 42–11 on the day. They smothered their opponent, choking them off as an MMA fighter would, waiting for the Czechs to tap out. Rostislav Olesz's short-handed goal 3:36 into the third came with Canada ahead 3–0. Glass would barely be tested the rest of the game.

"We have been preaching mental toughness from day one, no matter whether we're up a goal, or down a goal," said Sutter, whose team never trailed in the tournament. "You [media] guys have been talking about us playing easy games, but we haven't ever taken it easy. They played us tough today, and we knew they would."

As the clock wound down to triple zeroes and the Canadian players poured over the boards to congratulate each other, a mixed bag of feelings crept over the club. For some, it was that feeling of a job near completion. But for the twelve who had been in Helsinki the year before, when Fleury's gaffe had ended up in the net behind him, there was still a modicum of apprehension—this was their last chance for a gold medal.

"It's been a long time coming since last year," Jeff Carter said that day. "It's been in the back of our minds from the start of camp."

The funny thing about a World Juniors tournament is that you can have five or six teams all operating in their own vacuums. The Czechs are listening to the Czech press, and the Russians hear only what the Russian media has to say. Not that teams are completely ignorant of what's going around the tournament, but the party line back in Stockholm, Prague, or Moscow sometimes doesn't make it intact all the way to Thief River Falls.

"Everybody talked about how these [Canadian] kids were all playing in junior hockey, and we had guys who were already playing in the Russian Super League," Russian goalie Anton Khudobin recalled, almost fourteen years after the 2005 tournament. "Everyone talked about how rich this Russian team was, how they're making a lot of money [playing pro hockey in Russia]."

"Everyone" being people back in Russia, apparently. Because no one in North Dakota was talking up the Russians as a team that was going to be better than Canada, even if Russia did have Alex Ovechkin and Evgeni Malkin on the roster.

"We know Canada has good forwards and a very strong defence," Ovechkin allowed back in 2005 after his Russians had dispatched the U.S. 7–2 in the other semifinal. "But no one knows about their goalie."

The seeds of doubt. There may have been foreign outliers trying to poke holes in Canada's rock-solid veneer, but even Khudobin began to get the feeling that his Russians were perhaps about to get their money's worth against Canada.

"I only knew that Patrice Bergeron had played in the NHL," he said. "Of course, I knew of Crosby, but he was really new at that time. Other guys? I knew Shawn Belle because everyone talked about how fast he was."

So much was new to a kid from Siberia, at his first-ever WJC and standing at the end of a long plank as the scheduled starter in the gold medal game. Khudobin was just eighteen and still in awe of some of the goalie equipment the other guys had.

"I remember seeing [American goalie] Al Montoya, and he was wearing this unbelievable gear," Khudobin said. "It was Heaton equipment. Everything was in the American colours. I'm like, 'Oooohhh, could I have that, too?'

"I went back to Russia and said to myself, 'If I want to play in the NHL, I have to go back there to get ready.' The next year I went to the Saskatoon Blades."

When Khudobin skated out of the tunnel at "the Ralph" on

January 5, 2005, he was greeted by the first honest-to-goodness sell-out of the tournament—11,862 giddy fans, the majority bedecked in Canadian red. They had come to see the coronation, to watch the greatest Canadian team ever to grace a World Junior Championship secure their gold medals. As an appetizer, they hoped to watch a Canadian team defeat the Russians in a gold medal game for the first time in WJC history.

So, how best to describe what happened next?

In the words of Ilya Bryzgalov, the Russian goalie in a 7–3 loss to Canada at the 2010 Vancouver Olympics, "They came out like gorillas out of a cage."

Five years before that, on a much smaller stage in a much smaller arena in a much smaller town, Khudobin's experience wasn't much different from Bryzgalov's.

"It was a really fast game, and they were shooting from everywhere—which I wasn't used to. I never played over here, and they were shooting bad angle shots even. From everywhere!" said Khudobin, a fun-loving hockey survivor. He was born in Ust-Kamenogorsk, Kazakhstan, raised in Siberia, drafted in the seventh round by Minnesota, and played with five NHL organizations by the age of thirty-two.

"We'd played the night before against the U.S., and they had a pretty good roster, too. But we beat them like crazy, 7–2," he said. "I was thinking to expect the same thing from Canada, but they were all over us. *Boom! Boom! Boom!* It was like a nightmare. Like I was sleeping. *Boom! Boom! Boom! Boom!*

"It was crazy how good they were," Khudobin marvelled. "I think we had only fourteen shots."

Ryan Getzlaf accepted a Jeff Carter drop pass and powered a thirty-five-foot slap shot past Khudobin on Canada's very first shot of the game, fifty-one seconds into the contest. You know how visiting teams talk about taking the crowd *out* of the game? Yeah. Getzlaf's goal did quite the opposite. Then, just as the people began using their seats at the Ralph Engelstad Arena, Danny Syvret put them on their feet again, making it 2–0 at the 8:00 mark.

"We had a really good start, put them behind the eight ball," said Montreal Canadiens captain Shea Weber. "They were a really good team, but we put them in a spot where they had to take some chances, trying to come back on us. We took it to 'em. One of our best games."

It was during this gold medal game that McGuire coined perhaps his most famous term: the Double Dion. Phaneuf stepped up at the Canadian blue-line to hit Russian forward Enver Lisin, who managed to see him coming and bounce off the Canadian defenceman at the last second. Phaneuf ricocheted off Lisin and caromed right into Russia's Dmitri Pestunov, sending him flying.

"It's a Double Dion!" shouted McGuire, right overtop of Gord Miller's call.

The game evolved into what every other game at the 2005 WJC had turned into, with Canada squeezing the oxygen out of their opponents. The disparity between the two clubs became more apparent as the game wore on, one group of players enjoying their superiority in almost every area, and the other coming to the realization that they could probably play this game ten times over and they might not win even once.

Canada would win that gold medal game 6–1, scoring the last four goals against a Russian team that simply knew it could not compete with that 1985 draft class.

"What I remember is the dominance of the team. If they did [lose a period] I can't remember it," said Steve Getzlaf, who has followed his son's career through two World Juniors, two World Championships, two Olympic Games, and a World Cup. "They were just in total control the whole time. They weren't there to blow teams away, they just played their game and if it turned out they scored quite a few goals, that's the way it was. The team was just so solid from top to bottom. And physical, too."

Canada just had too many tools, and one of those was the ability to physically eliminate whatever weapons the opponent required to compete. In this case, that weapon was Alexander Ovechkin.

Russia's best player was a Canadian target from the drop of the puck, and the top pair of Weber and Phaneuf made sure his head was on a swivel every time he hopped over the boards that night in Grand Forks. He would last around half a game, give or take a few shifts near the end where he was testing a shoulder that Team Canada had done a little handiwork on.

Eventually, Ovechkin just couldn't go anymore.

"We just played him hard, like every other team's top line," Weber said. "Our pairing was a physical one, and we wanted to play physical—especially on him. Limit time and space; don't give him room to make a play."

So, who gets the credit for knocking Ovechkin out of that gold medal final?

"I don't remember," Phaneuf said. You get the sense that he does, in fact, remember, and that it *was* him. But as a thousand-game NHL player, he long ago learned that a pro does not exhibit glee—or take credit—when an opposing player is injured.

Others were not quite so diplomatic.

Weber: "Yeah, it was a Dion hit. I'm sure Dion felt pretty good about himself."

Getzlaf: "I think people want to believe it was Dion, but I think it was Perr's [Corey Perry's]. I don't think there was anyone who was going to intimidate our roster at that point."

Sutter: "It was Dion and someone else. He got hit by one person, then the other. Dion got him, and as soon as he got up he got drilled again. And he was done."

Glass: "I think it was two hits. I think it might have been Colin Fraser, to be honest."

McGuire: "Anyone who was within a stick's length of Ovechkin got a piece of him, but I think it was Bergeron who got him with the crushing blow."

Bergeron: "I don't think it was me. I had a hit on him that game, but there were so many guys that hit him that I couldn't tell you. I don't know. I wondered if it was Phaneuf, because he hit some guys in the middle, but I don't know if it's him."

Phaneuf: "I think it wasn't just one hit. It was a few different hits. We had to key in on him, and we were physical on him. We took him out of the game, which was an obvious advantage for us. But we played a physical brand of hockey the whole tournament."

Khudobin couldn't tell you who delivered the telling blow, but he had a front row seat for the aftermath.

"I was sitting in the hallway next to the bench," said the Russian goalie, who had been pulled before the halfway point in the game, "and he came skating toward me. 'Fuck! Fuck! Fuck!' He stayed there and tried to recover, but he couldn't play."

After the game, the Canadians loaded into a bus and went straight back to Winnipeg. They had early morning flights back to their junior clubs, their two-week Dream Team experience feeling exactly that way—as though it had been a dream.

After the tournament, the local paper in Grand Forks lamented the unmet expectations of local businesses, as well as the complaints of locals who had bought tournament packages only to be undercut by the aftermarket, once it became clear there would be a plenitude of empty seats. At the same time, organizers of the following year's tournament in Vancouver were bragging about eleven thousand tournament packages having already been sold, while predicting sellouts of every single game the next year. The Canadian hockey circus had rolled through Grand Forks, complete with its own fans and the greatest team most North Dakotans never saw, and left with the hardware.

"I look back on that team and it would be the best team I . . ." said Phaneuf, before stopping midsentence. "I look back on that team and the biggest compliment is that people say it was the best World Juniors team ever. To be a part of that as a player, it's a pretty big honour.

"I have a big bond with those guys. Always will."

CHAPTER 8

Once in a Generation

"At an age where guys shouldn't be that dominant, in a tournament like that, Crosby was."

—SHEA WEBER

Only seven players have pulled on a Team Canada sweater at the World Juniors at the tender age of sixteen: Wayne Gretzky, Sidney Crosby, Connor McDavid, Eric Lindros, Jason Spezza, Jay Boumeester, and young Bill Campbell, who went to the tournament in 1981 with Dale Hawerchuk's Cornwall Royals, but alas, never played in the National Hockey League.

Statistics tell us that kids born in the first quarter of a given year get drafted into the NHL nearly three times as often as kids born in any quarter after that. Now, extrapolate that to kids in their teenage years, where the difference in a full year of development, growth, and strength is like 400 metres of track in a 1,500-metre race.

A sixteen-year-old at the World Juniors? That, my friend, is a tall order.

"It was a big step, no question," said Crosby, who played in Helsinki in 2004, a good seven months before his seventeenth birthday. "You're sixteen, and your game isn't even close to where the eighteen- and nineteen-year-olds' are. And your body isn't close to where those guys are. I still felt confident, but I knew there were a lot of other guys who had a more mature game and were ready for that level, more so than I was."

As a sixteen-year-old in his first Under-20 tournament, Crosby had two goals and five points—tied for the third-best performance by a sixteen-year-old in WJC history. But no matter how impressive Crosby's performance, he would inevitably be compared to one name that came before his: Wayne Gretzky.

Gretzky arrived in Montreal in 1978, in a time before sports channels and YouTube highlights. Gretzky's production in his first World Juniors would be more than three times that of Crosby in his first appearance, and Gretzky would become to sixteen-year-olds at the WJC exactly what he became to all NHL players: the best there ever was.

At the time, however, Gretzky was simply this mythical kid from Brantford, Ontario, who was on his way to a 70-goal and 182-point OHL season playing in Sault Ste. Marie. He wasn't invited to the World Juniors summer camp in Orillia, Ontario, and when Gretzky arrived in Montreal that winter of 1978, he walked into a dressing room housing names like Ryan Walter, Tony McKegney, Brad Marsh, Craig Hartsburg, Rick Vaive, Stan Smyl, Bobby Smith, Brad "Sarge" McCrimmon, and Steve Tambellini.

"There were fifteen guys on that team who played over five

hundred NHL games. Seven over one thousand. *Seven over one thousand games,*" marvelled Steve Tambellini. "Those are all significant careers. Then you add Gretz. How does that team ever lose?"

Gretzky was still a kid back then. Mousy, humble, barely said a thing. The CTV's Ron Reusch worked him for five minutes in a live television interview and barely got enough quotes for a sidebar. It was like a guy breaking up cement with an ice pick.

But when the games started, that sixteen-year-old was the best player on the ice—times ten. The problem was, in that cathedral of hockey known as the Montreal Forum, there weren't many in the pews to bear witness.

"The Forum is one of my favourite places of all time," Tambellini said. "Just to sit down and have a coffee, let alone to play hockey. But when we walked out [of the dressing room], it was different. There were only a couple of thousand people there.

"Looking back, people had an idea of the significance of what was happening with the World Juniors. It was 'pre-' this incredible show that people see every Christmastime now, but the players felt the same walking on to that ice with a Canadian jersey, I can tell you that."

It was only the second "official" IIHF U-20 tournament, after the three "unofficial" ones from 1974 to 1976 and the first "official" tournament held in Czechoslovakia in 1977. Canadians just didn't know what this thing was about, and the fact that the inhabitants of one of the most knowledgeable hockey cities in the history of hockey weren't flocking to see the Gretzky kid . . . well, that tells you how slowly word got around in those days.

Tambellini first met Gretzky while checking into their Montreal hotel.

"We're all young, but he's this sixteen-year-old. He says, 'Steve,

Wayne Gretzky.' I say, 'Yeah, I know who *you* are.' But a lot of us had not actually seen him play," Tabellini recounted. "Everybody knew he was a fabulous player. He was sixteen coming to play with us. So we practiced a few times, and you know what practice is like. You can always tell at practice which guys are the fastest skaters or the best shooters. But it's always different when it's game-on."

Canada's first game was against the Americans.

"When the lights came on, it was, 'Wow. What are we watching here?'" Tambellini said. "He was so far ahead, in his mind, of where most everyone else was thinking. And execution? Even though maybe some people might be able to tell what he was going to do, he still could execute under pressure.

"I remember playing the Russians, and I was on a line with Curt Fraser and Stan Smyl. We were sitting on the bench, and he scored a goal where we just sat there and looked at each other. I said, 'That might be the best goal I've ever seen.' He was doing things, at age sixteen, that nobody else in the tournament could do. We were not laughing on the bench, but we couldn't believe we had such great seats to see what he was doing."

Gretzky would lead the tournament with 17 points in six games, 6 points more than the next-most-productive sixteen-year-old in WJC history (Robert Reichel), and 12 points up on third place—future Edmonton Oilers teammate Reijo Ruotsalainen, and Crosby, who each had 5 points.

The year that Gretzky made his World Juniors debut, Bob McKenzie was a twenty-two-year-old Leafs fan who would get his first big job at the *Sault Star* the following summer.

"I can always remember being at my uncle's house on Boxing Day 1977, and the game was on national television: Canada versus Czechoslovakia. It was the Wayne Gretzky show," McKenzie said in his podcast, *The TSN Hockey Bobcast*. "If you've never seen the highlights of Wayne Gretzky versus the Czechs in 1977, look it up. Because he just danced his way through the Czechoslovakian team. It was insane, what this Gretzky kid was doing."

Gretzky had 3 goals and 3 assists in the game against Czechoslovakia. It was Canada's introduction to the greatest offensive player the sport of hockey would ever see.

"I'd been aware of him, you read stories about him, you'd heard about him," McKenzie said. "But that was the first time I ever saw Wayne Gretzky play, as it was for many Canadians.

"What he did in that game against players who were far older and far bigger . . . When you saw him, he looked so small. And skinny. He looked totally out of place—until the puck was dropped. Then he just dominated. He took the game completely over."

Fast-forward over a quarter century, and you can imagine how much more aware everyone was of the kid from Cole Harbour, Nova Scotia, when Sidney Crosby pulled into the summer evaluation camp before the 2004 World Juniors in Helsinki. Crosby's 5 points didn't make near the impact that Gretzky's 17 did, but when Crosby and Team Canada lost to the U.S.A. on that Marc-Andre Fleury carom off Braydon Coburn, Crosby returned the following summer not just as a seventeen-year-old under-ager, but as a veteran with a chip on his shoulder.

"As a coach, you just looked at him and saw a star. A guy who would be your best player," said 2005 head coach Brent Sutter. "He was responsible, hard to knock off pucks. In practice, Sidney treated every drill like it was a game situation. You could see that he wanted to be first in every drill, and he hated to lose."

To hear Crosby tell the story, he was just trying to survive at a summer selection camp that was loaded with players who were still perturbed about losing in Helsinki.

"I remember that summer camp, in August in Calgary. It was so competitive, so intense, for a team that was mostly returning guys. A lot of that was Sutter. He made sure guys came in with the right mindset," Crosby said.

Sutter, meanwhile, could see a relationship forming between Crosby and Patrice Bergeron, who was a little more than two years Crosby's senior. Bergeron was playing in the American Hockey League during that lockout season, but as the lockout extended past the Christmas break, Boston allowed Bergeron to leave the AHL and play at the WJC. Sutter quickly made the two roommates.

"I was just trying to take that next step," Crosby said of his second World Juniors. "Having the same guys there I felt pretty comfortable, even though I was still one of the younger guys. We got to Gimli [Manitoba], and Bergeron was my roommate. I just remember asking him a hundred questions about what it was like playing in the NHL the year before. I picked his brain a lot, annoyed him. I was just trying to make the most of the experience."

As with Gretzky, it didn't take long before Crosby's teammates started to realize that there was something special going on with this player. Sid was seventeen, and already he was doing things that the nineteen-year-olds couldn't do.

"Everyone knew he was supposed to be 'the Next One' coming out of junior," said defenceman Shea Weber. "We all heard how good he was, how good he was supposed to be. But just being able to play with him, watch him, on a daily basis, we learned how good he actually was.

"At an age where guys shouldn't be that dominant, in a tournament like that, he was."

Goalie Jeff Glass had his Sidney Crosby moment when the team was at their pretournament retreat in Gimli.

"There wasn't a lot of media coverage—that was part of the point of getting away," Glass said. "And he got on the ice before there were any cameras in the building, and he was practicing a few moves that I had never seen before. I remember asking him why he didn't do it in a game. He said, 'I couldn't. It would be showboating, and it wouldn't go over well.'

"I just couldn't wrap my head around how he had the talent to do those things, but he was very mindful of the fact there was a time and a place [for] handling the puck the way he was. I've never seen skill like that in practice.

"It's something where I get to say I had a front row seat—better than a front row seat—to see Sid Crosby play the World Juniors. It was my first taste of the way he could just take over a game. He was still young, but he found a way to be noticeable every game and every practice. It was my first glimpse at a real superstar. It was really, really cool."

This will come as no surprise, but as the older players watched this seventeen-year-old emerging as the next generational player, they were also witnessing a young man who already knew how to handle everything that comes with that stardom.

"I saw a humble guy, especially for all the accolades and expectations that he had on his shoulders at that point," Weber said. "He was very down to earth. A humble kid for sure. Definitely nice to see that."

Crosby, like Gretzky before him and McDavid after, has had almost a flawless record in the media. Almost.

It was before that 2005 tournament in North Dakota—with the NHL lockout threatening to rage into the following season—that TSN's Geno Reda asked Crosby if he'd play in the NHL the following season if the players were still locked out.

"I think if I do have the opportunity, I would probably go," opined the young superstar, oblivious to the shock waves that quote would send through the hockey world.

Some weeks before, Crosby's agent, Pat Brisson, had stated, "There's no way he'll be a replacement player." Now he watched as his BlackBerry exploded with reactions to Crosby's misguided comment. National Hockey League Players' Association head Bob Goodenow was undoubtedly one of those who dialed Brisson's number that day, so it was no coincidence that Crosby was ready the following day with an about-face.

"If there is an NHL with replacement players, I think for me to be involved and to say that I would play in the league is not true," Crosby said. "If the NHL is the real NHL with the best players in the world, for sure I want to play in it. But at the same time, if it's a league of replacement players, it's not the real NHL. And with all the things going on right now with players and owners, it's not right and I don't think I'd be playing in a league like that."

Asked about the incident today, Crosby laughs. It seems a million years ago, but truly, it is one of his rare few missteps in the media.

"That was a tough decision as a kid," he said. "Your dream is to play in the NHL. You don't expect that scenario, and it's incredible to think how that worked out with the [draft] lottery and how that all shaped up.

"The kid inside of you, who has been dreaming all these years of playing in the NHL, that's what he thought. He wanted to be in the NHL."

After having played in Helsinki the year before, Crosby was ascending to rock star status in a hockey-mad country like Canada. There was so much hype around the 2005 team in North Dakota, they were already calling it the best roster ever assembled for a World Juniors. Even though many of the good citizens of Grand Forks and

Thief River Falls might not have known of the legend of Crosby, thousands of Canadians—and all the Canadian players—surely did.

"When he came into that '05 tournament, it was a Tiger Woods–like presence," said Ryan Getzlaf, then a nineteen-year-old centre-man on the team. "There was a different atmosphere, a different following when he was around. It was fun. It created a lot of buzz and excitement in that building, and going into it."

Canada rode cleanly to a gold medal game against Russia, where they blitzed the Russians 6–1. It was the perfect way for Crosby to end his time at the U-20 level, as Canada ran roughshod over Alex Ovechkin, Crosby's future Penguins teammate Evgeni Malkin, and the rest of Team Russia.

"You're young and so full of energy. You want it so bad—especially losing the year before," Crosby said. "We were a year older, more mature. I just don't remember anyone passing up a hit. I probably had the most hits I'd ever had, in that game.

"I remember Sutter making sure the message was really clear: We had some skill, but we had to play a physical game. Between Webs and Dion, we had some heavy, heavy defencemen."

That gold medal, despite the Stanley Cups and Olympic golds he has won, still has a special place in Crosby's heart.

"You dreamed of that," he said. "You don't know if you're going to play in the NHL at that point. Honestly, the NHL was not even on my mind. I was thinking that this was the chance of a lifetime to be at the World Juniors, something I'd watched on TV every year. I had great memories of getting up early when it was overseas.

"You're just a Canadian kid trying to make a dream come true. That's how I looked at it."

Crosby was it. He was the kid that the Program of Excellence was supposed to produce—identified as a fifteen-year-old, and then promoted level by level within the ecosystem. Of course, he was a generational talent. But the path was in place for him, and others like him, to make the most of the talents that were bestowed upon them.

Crosby had come from one of the tiny hockey corners of Canada, but had no trouble making his way through the minor systems, to elite level kids' hockey, and eventually to the Program of Excellence. If a Crosby could be found in tiny Cole Harbour, then there wasn't a corner of the Canadian hockey world that could hide a potential national teamer.

"Whether it's grassroots, with your minor hockey coaches, or the opportunity to play on a provincial team," Crosby said. "We were all in small towns [across Nova Scotia], and the league wasn't a provincial league. So when they invited you to come play, you were seeing a bunch of different guys—bigger, faster, stronger guys. Then you go to Atlantics, and the same thing happens.

"Then you get to the national level—you're talking Air Canada Cup and Midget AAA nationals—and all of those steps become learning curves."

And then one day, that kid from Cole Harbour, Nova Scotia, finds himself on an Olympic rink in Vancouver yelling, "Iggy!" And scoring the Golden Goal.

"It's really neat," Crosby said. "And I don't think the coaches you have at a young age get enough credit, because they are the ones who instill a lot of different qualities in us as players. And in Canada, there's no shortage of those people. There are tons of guys willing to spend the time to help kids, and I was happy to have that back home."

In 2014 in Malmö, Sweden, it was Connor McDavid's turn. By that time, we were well into a social media world that harbours no secrets. McDavid was the lone sixteen-year-old on that team, stocked with names like Jonathan Drouin, Anthony Mantha, Zach Fucale, and a seventeen-year-old Aaron Ekblad. Still, McDavid was anything but under the radar for Canadian fans, who had not seen a World Juniors gold medal since 2009.

Hockey Canada brought Brent Sutter back that year to coach his third WJC, in hopes of getting back to the mojo that had made Canada the dominant nation at the U-20 level. That winning culture had been slipping in the years leading up to McDavid's debut in Malmö, and he would find that the screws would be pinned down tightly by Sutter.

"We played in Malmö, and we had a huge group of Canadians travel over," McDavid recalled. "We were in the smaller venue—Sweden was in the big one—and I just remember our rink being packed with Canadians. And as the tournament went on, there were more, and more, and more Canadians showing up. So for me, it felt like a Canadian World Juniors, only away from Canada."

McDavid started on a line with Bo Horvat and Sam Reinhart, and he felt he played well in Canada's opener against Germany.

"We had a good game, the team won and our line was good," he said. "Then we played the Czechs, I took a couple of penalties, and found myself as the thirteenth forward. I was the thirteenth forward the rest of the tournament."

Connor McDavid? The thirteenth forward? It couldn't be.

"I don't know if he was our thirteenth forward," Sutter said, hedging a bit. "But as the tournament went on, there was just a young player who was overwhelmed in it. Yet, you knew he was going to be a star. A player who would lead a World Juniors team at some point."

Alas, "some point" wasn't "that point" for McDavid. Not quite yet. So he humbly played when and where he was asked, the youngest Canadian player being made by Sutter to take one for the team.

"I definitely had a different kind of experience. An experience where I wasn't a top-line player. I still played powerplay and whatnot, but I wasn't as relied on there," McDavid said. He had always played on teams with older players, but at no other point had he been counted on less to lead his team. "I think I started playing house league with five-year-olds when I was four. I've been playing above my age group since I was a little, little guy.

"I'm not going to lie. I didn't enjoy my first World Juniors experience," McDavid admitted. "I didn't have a lot of fun with it. My team, we didn't perform at our best. We came in fourth."

Hockey Canada's plan in bringing in Sutter went hand in hand with having eleven players who would be eligible to return in 2015. It was wise planning, as they had a superior team in 2015, a returning coach, and a bunch of hungry returnees, as much as with Crosby's second crack at gold in North Dakota.

"When we came home and played, we played in the Bell Centre and the Air Canada Centre. As a Canadian kid, those are *the* rinks you want to play in," McDavid said. "We were such a good team. We never trailed at all in that tournament. If it wasn't for a lull, we would have beaten Russia four, five, six to one."

Yes, we've been meaning to ask. What the heck happened in that nervous gold medal game?

Canada led 2–1 after twenty minutes, then added 3 more goals by the 12:30 mark of the second period.

"We were up 5–1, and they scored a couple quick ones," McDavid said. "Then they get a powerplay, and they score. Then they get another powerplay and score. All of the sudden it's 5–4 going into the third, and we're, like, 'What the heck's going on?'"

Luckily, the Canadians were able to settle down. After Russia scored those 3 goals in the final 5:39 of the second period, Team

Canada nursed their 5–4 lead through a scoreless third period to claim the gold.

McDavid had 3 goals and 8 assists in the tournament, tying him with Nic Petan and Sam Reinhart—both of whom were two years older—for the tournament scoring lead. A decade after Crosby had introduced himself to Canadians in Grand Forks, and some thirty-seven years after Gretzky's only appearance, McDavid left his Canadian teammates with the distinct impression that they had met a guy who had some serious, serious talent.

"I remember Connor's [presence] being some added attention, some added pressure," said Soo defenceman Darnell Nurse. "Especially because the World Juniors the year before hadn't gone that great. We were back in Toronto and Montreal, and you had the 'seekers' outside the hotel, trying to get Connor's autograph."

Nurse had played against McDavid in the OHL, where McDavid was an Erie Otter. But this wasn't the same deal.

"Until you play with him each and every night, you don't realize how special he is," said Nurse, who has been McDavid's teammate, roommate at times, and close friend in McDavid's first four NHL seasons in Edmonton. "You try to make up a game plan to defend him, and most of the time it doesn't work. But when he's on your team, every single night, he does something that wows you. Even to this day. The first I saw it was playing with him at the World Juniors."

This is what we've always heard about trying to figure out who are the good and who are the not-so-good players: The players always know first.

Coaches, GMs, agents, and hockey writers—they all have opinions.

But players? Give them a few practices, maybe a game or two with a guy, and they'll tell you how good he really is. Or if he isn't any good at all.

That's why guys like Gretzky, Crosby, and McDavid get so much respect around the league. It's the respect of their peers—the best kind of praise for any of us, no matter what we do for a living.

"They're elite for a reason," Nurse said. "Connor would dominate every practice, whether it's one-on-ones or playing five-on-five. I remember one time in practice, it was a one-on-three and he went through three guys. It was his first year here in Edmonton."

Today, McDavid is either the best player in the world, or the second, after Crosby, depending on who you talk to. And like Crosby, he is a product of the Program of Excellence.

We all hope that the NHL will return to sending players to the Winter Olympics, and do so in time for McDavid and Crosby to work a powerplay together. Would it be like Gretzky and Lemieux in that 1987 Canada Cup? We can only imagine the pedigree of hockey those two could create together.

McDavid, for one, would love to find out. It would be the icing on the cake for a young superstar who knows the Program of Excellence is a part of who he is today.

"Some of my favourite hockey that I've ever played has come in a Canadian jersey," McDavid said. "And some of the games you want to forget have come in a Hockey Canada jersey. So, you get the highs and the lows of hockey, and you learn from that. As a player and a person.

"I have lots of friends who I met in a Hockey Canada jersey who I would have no business knowing. Absolutely, it's made me a better person."

CHAPTER 9

Have Pads, Will Travel

"I'm proud of the way I did it.
It wasn't conventional, that's for sure."

—JEFF GLASS

Justin Pogge was sitting in a Vancouver hotel room with Steve Downie, praying for silence.

For a couple of teenagers travelling the junior hockey circuit, the room was nicer than any hotel room they would overnight in all season. But it was a kamikaze's comfort, their plush surroundings undermined by the mental torture that was cut-down day for Team Canada at a World Juniors.

The final camp for the 2006 World Juniors team had wrapped up the day before, and the Team Canada routine had been explained to every potential roster player. "If your hotel phone rang, that meant one of you was cut and you had to go to an exit meeting," Pogge said. "If you don't get the phone call, you've made the team."

So that morning in that Vancouver hotel room, Downie, a winger from Newmarket, Ontario, and Pogge, a goalie who did most of his growing up in Penticton, B.C., tried nervously to chat, or read, or watch some TV. Whatever it took for that hour or so to pass, they coexisted like a couple of nervous kids on a first date.

Fortunately for both players, their hotel room phone never rang that day. But that morning became part of the tapestry for Pogge, a guy who seemed never to have anything handed to him. He became one of a litany of Canadian World Juniors goalies whose dreams unfolded—but not quite the way you'd have thought they might after a Christmas in the crease for Team Canada.

One season before Pogge tended Team Canada's nets, the job had gone to Jeff Glass, another Western Hockey League goalie with a bit of a history. Glass had been passed over in the WHL's Bantam Draft, subsequently listed by the Tri-City Americans (they simply claimed his rights as an undrafted junior), and then dealt to Kootenay. Eventually, at the National Hockey League's 2004 Entry Draft, Glass would be chosen eighty-ninth by Ottawa—one spot before Toronto selected Justin Pogge.

The pair never played together, but their careers would mirror one another for years to come.

"I certainly wasn't on Hockey Canada's radar at all," Glass said. "I didn't do any Under-16, Under-17. No World Juniors summer camp for me. Didn't get an invite."

Not everyone was a Patrice Bergeron, a Shea Weber, or a Sidney Crosby on that 2005 team in North Dakota. There were guys named Shawn Belle, Jeremy Colliton, Stephen Dixon, and Rejean Beauchemin on that roster as well. But Glass's dream was to play in a World Juniors, and this was his last chance. So he set himself a goal to get noticed. He started by playing his rear end off every time his Kootenay Ice played the Red Deer Rebels, who were coached by Team Canada coach Brent Sutter. It worked—Glass managed an invite to the Canada-Russia CHL Series and seized the opportunity, posting a shutout while playing in Sutter's arena in Red Deer.

By December, Glass had wormed his way into Team Canada's final training camp. He was sent on his way by Kootenay Ice owner Ed Chynoweth, one of the key figures in the formation of the Program of Excellence.

"I remember Ed bringing Nigel Dawes and me into his office one day, right before the World Juniors, to tell us how lucky we were to get to go to camp, and wishing us the best," Glass said. "When he called you into his office, it was pretty cool. He commanded a lot of respect."

The other goalies at that Winnipeg camp were Kamloops Blazer Devan Dubnyk, Kevin Nastiuk of the Medicine Hat Tigers, and the Winnipeg-born Beauchemin of the Prince Albert Raiders. Four WHL guys, each of whom Glass knew well.

"I knew I was the least popular goalie on that list, and I was going to have to play really well to earn a spot," Glass said. "I was the last guy, probably, on most media lists. But I knew three-quarters of the way through camp that I was playing noticeably well, and I had another shutout in an exhibition game. I don't know if I was supposed to hear this or not, but I heard through Nigel Dawes where Brent had said, 'If he keeps doing what he's doing, he'll be just fine.' Nigel told me, 'I think Brent likes you.'"

Glen Glass, Jeff's father, is an engineer in the oil and gas industry. When Glass was younger, his mom, Jane, stayed home, taking care of three kids and making the Glass home in Calgary. Trevor Glass, Jeff's younger brother, played in Spokane for the WHL Chiefs, where he won a Memorial Cup. You've seen him on national TV—he was the player about to accept the Memorial Cup trophy from team captain Chris Bruton when the trophy busted off the base. "That's what he's famous for," Jeff said, laughing. "He's on the blooper reel every year."

The elder Glass would find his window of fame elsewhere, playing behind the best Canadian roster ever to be assembled at a World Juniors.

"I kind of got the ball in camp, and I never really let it go. I knew I'd get one chance to do my thing, and I wasn't going to let anyone else get into the net," he said. "Next thing you know, I made the team. That was the hardest part, with that team. I knew that once I was on it, we'd have a pretty good chance of winning."

Pogge never knew his father, and his mom did whatever it took to give her son the opportunities in life she thought he deserved. That meant moving now and again to pursue her career. So the kid was born in Fort McMurray, Alberta, then lived some in Calgary, before calling Penticton, British Columbia, his hometown. It's where he played his minor league hockey, and where he returned after being cut by the Western Hockey League's Prince George Cougars, playing Junior B hockey in nearby Summerland.

Like Glass, Pogge was never drafted into the WHL. The Cougars did list him, though, and that's about as good as it got for Pogge. He made the team on his second try, playing forty-four games behind a sub-.500 Cougars club that included a young defenceman named Dustin Byfuglien. Pogge would eventually be dealt to the Calgary Hitmen, halfway through the 2004–05 campaign. "And that's where everything kind of picked up," he said. "Playing with a little confidence, playing with a little bit better team. Just maturing, through my second and third years in that league."

The problem was that Pogge's maturation as a Major Junior goaltender wasn't in step with his window to realize his life-long dream of playing in the World Juniors. He'd been on Hockey Canada's radar as a younger player, but in his eighteen-year-old season, Pogge's numbers were simply okay. And "okay" doesn't get a guy an invite to Hockey Canada's World Juniors summer camp.

During his time in Calgary, however, Pogge had become familiar with young Jeff Glass, who had taken a similarly circuitous route that had landed him between the pipes of Canada's World Juniors team the year before. So, for once in his hockey career, Pogge had a solid nugget of good fortune in his mental holster—an example of what can happen if you work hard, believe, and maybe toss a few pennies into the right fountain along the way.

"We both didn't get invited to their summer camps. We weren't on their radar," Pogge said of Glass and himself. "I was so pumped with how it went for Glasser the year before, and Jeff had a conversation with me that year. He said, 'Just be the best goalie so they have to take you.' I had it in my head that I wanted to make the team. The [2006] tournament was in Vancouver, my home province, and I would think about it before all of my games. I really focused in—even put a wish up on a Chinese Wishing Tree."

If you've ever seen a Chinese Wishing Tree, you'd know it looks like a fruit tree that should have been harvested two weeks ago.

Hundreds of little tags that represent the dreams of hundreds of people. A thousand wishes that mostly turn out to be just that—a wish. A hope.

Brent Sutter would require more than that from his World Juniors goaltender.

Playing goal behind Team Canada in North Dakota was like riding Secretariat in 1973 or caddying for Tiger Woods in the early 2000s. Glass just had to stay in the saddle, or keep up, and there would be a trophy waiting at the end of the line.

"We were heading up to Gimli, Manitoba, for a pretournament [bonding exercise], and I remember looking around the bus after I'd made the team, and thinking, 'Every guy is a surefire NHLer,'" Glass said. "Some of the most fun memories I have of that team are from practice, because you can imagine the guys who were shooting it."

The practices were physical for Glass. But the games? He could have played two-thirds of his periods in a rocking chair. They were more of a mental exercise.

"It's been tough on our goaltender when we've only given up 10, 12, 15 shots a game," said Sutter at the time. "After the second period [of the semifinal], the Czechs only had 1 shot on goal from inside our blue-line. But I mean, would you rather be facing 40 shots a game or play behind a team that's only giving up 11?"

Glass would allow just 7 goals all tournament long, but he had a saves percentage of only .922—that's how few shots he faced.

Team Canada bused from Grand Forks, North Dakota, to Winnipeg right after the gold medal game. "Within hours I was on a plane back to Cranbrook," Glass said.

It would be a long time before Glass saw a lot of those teammates again.

"That was my year," Pogge says of the 2005–06 campaign. "It just ended up being a World Juniors year."

That's the thing about the highest level of sports. Only the elite few get there and stay there, year after year. For the thousands of others who try, there are momentary spikes that cannot be sustained, ceilings that can't be exceeded, and levels where they simply get left behind by the competition. Take, for example, the term "a good AHL goalie." Do you know how good you have to be to become known as "a good AHL goalie"? In the end, however, that goalie never gets rich. Worse yet, in some obtuse way he has failed in his goal to make the NHL.

For every Carey Price who plays more than a decade in the NHL, there are how many hundreds of goalies whose talents could not get them past bantam, past university hockey, past the East Coast League, or past a cup of coffee as an NHL backup? No one has a deeper read on this than Pogge, who chuckled at the fact that the best statistical year of his hockey career happened as a nineteen-year-old in Calgary.

"I was 38-10-6, with a 1.72 goals against and 11 shutouts," he said. "That's a pretty good season. I wish I could draw back into that a little bit. I wouldn't mind one of those again."

It was the kind of season that could make a guy a walk-on at Team Canada's December camp, after not even being on the invite list the prior summer. "It was a dream come true, just getting asked to come to the training camp. I was nervous the whole time. I didn't know I was going to be our guy. I mean, we had Carey Price in camp."

Price was eighteen at the time and would get his chance the following year in Leksand and Mora, Sweden. Pogge's partner in Vancouver would turn out to be Devan Dubnyk. The two had been goalies on Canada's U-18 team together and won the eye of Sutter, who had returned after leading Glass's 2005 team to gold.

"We were all scared of him," Pogge said of Sutter, with a laugh. "He's a great guy but he's just this ominous figurehead. I love the guy. He actually caught me dancing before a pregame skate one time. He just shook his head."

While Dubnyk, barring the unforeseen, will have played his five hundredth NHL regular-season game sometime in the fall of 2019, he didn't get a minute of crease time in Vancouver that year. Sutter rode Pogge for every minute of that World Juniors, and Pogge rewarded his coach by allowing just 6 goals in the four-game preliminary round. One fewer than Glass had.

But there was a subplot in Vancouver that ran the whole tournament long, revolving around two goalies who were both property of the Toronto Maple Leafs: Finland's Tuukka Rask, a first-rounder drafted twenty-first overall by Toronto in 2005, and Pogge, chosen by the Leafs in the third round in 2004.

"Rask and Pogge both had the physical attributes to be number-one pro goaltenders," said John Ferguson, Jr., the Leafs' GM in 2006. "Through junior, and with Pogge's performance at the World Juniors, he certainly did project to be an NHL number one or, at worst, a two."

Anyone who follows hockey in Canada can imagine the hype machine that was churning that December and January in Vancouver, as not one but *two* Maple Leafs properties were tearing up the World Juniors in goal. Pogge would prove the top goalie in the WJC field and Rask ranked third by the end of the tournament—thanks mostly to his team's two losses to Canada. The top five goalies at the tournament were Pogge, Swede Daniel Larsson, Rask, Russian Anton Khudobin, and Cory Schneider of the U.S. Rask was named the All-Star goalie by the media and the Goalie of the Tournament by the IIHF Tournament Directorate.

"I liked the way he played, but really, I just wanted gold," Pogge said with a shrug. "I had just signed with Toronto, another milestone and a dream come true. I didn't have any issue with who was who, or who was next. He was another guy in the system, and I was going to see him at camp. But, I never saw him at camp."

As it turned out, the pair were two ships passing in the night. Two young men who, in the short term, were simply trying to stop the next puck that was flying their way, while trying to find a living in the game in the longer term—no matter what jersey they would be asked to pull over their chest protectors every night.

"I didn't hear a lot about him," Rask said of Pogge. "It was obvious, when we were in the same tournament and the same team's property, people were talking. But the Finnish media wasn't talking about that. Once we got to Canada, it wasn't like I was watching TSN all the time, looking for my name up there."

'Twas ever thus. The media's fixation, or story angles that fans devour, are often the furthest topics from the minds of the players themselves. Honestly, do you think either guy cared even a little bit about the goalie at other end of the ice? Maybe if he were shooting pucks at him, sure. But from what I've gathered in my years of writing hockey, the goalies are usually cheering for each other to succeed.

Pogge and Rask met in the tournament opener for both teams, in front of a sold-out house at the old Pacific Coliseum, the former home of the Vancouver Canucks that was the 2006 home of the WHL's Giants. It was a rude awakening for the Finns.

"Against Latvia and the Slovaks, the games weren't so tough," said

Finnish goal scorer Aki Seitsonen, a strapping young Calgary Flames draft pick who never quite panned out. "Not like this."

Welcome to a World Juniors in Canada, son.

Canada won 5–1, coming at Rask with a methodical attack for period leads of 2–0 and 4–0. The shots were 31–17, and with the win, Pogge and his mates were on their way. They sleepwalked past Switzerland 4–3, beat Norway 4–0, and then ran the preliminary round table with a 3–2 win over the U.S. That bought Canada a seat in the semifinal, awaiting the winner of a Finland-Sweden quarterfinal that was "seventh game of the Stanley Cup" stuff back home for both teams.

When Teemu Laakso pinched in from the point to fire home a rebound with thirty-four seconds remaining in overtime, the Nashville draft pick lifted underdog Finland to a 1–0 victory, denying the Swedes a shot at Canada the following night. Sweden had outshot Finland 53–25, but the legend of Tuukka grew a full metre that night in Vancouver, as he carried little Finland to victory over its big brother and neighbour, Sweden.

"In one hockey game when you fight really hard and you have excellent goalkeeping, anything can happen," said Finnish head coach Hannu Aravirta.

Added his Swedish counterpart, Torgny Bendelin: "I have been in the game for twenty-seven years. This is the toughest loss I have ever had. The team just couldn't play better. I tell you, the team and the players, they're devastated."

The Canadian media, however, was delighted to have a Pogge-Rask, winner-take-all semifinal to pump. In what had become somewhat of a referendum—at least for the Eastern Canadian media—the game would settle which of the two goalies should be favoured for a long career as the Maple Leafs starter. The big Canadian with the quiet game, who didn't see many pucks but allowed very few to get past? Or the handsome Finn, who was by necessity more acrobatic, and oh so much fun to watch tend the Suomi nets?

Twenty-four hours later, the Canadians had ripped four pucks past Rask, defeating the Finns 4–0. It was a cold, calculating win by a superior team, and a game in which nobody could really credit the goaltender on either side for having affected the outcome in any major way.

In the years since, Rask has become the all-time winningest goalie in Bruins history, passing names like Cecil "Tiny" Thompson, Frank Brimsek, Gerry Cheevers, and Tim Thomas. He has seen enough in his years to know one thing about that Canada-Finland matchup.

"We didn't have a chance," Rask says now. "Our offence wasn't close to what Canada had. It was tough to beat Canada on their home soil—especially in a semifinal game. But we ended up beating the U.S. in the bronze medal game, so that made up for it."

Rask has won a Stanley Cup as a backup in 2011, and he played in another as a starter two years later, losing in six games to Chicago. He played for the Suomi in three World Juniors from 2005 to 2007, but relished his opportunity to experience a Canadian WJC.

"Being eighteen or nineteen, and you are playing in an NHL arena in front of eighteen thousand people, it's something that is pretty amazing, that you've never experienced before. And a lot of guys will never experience that again."

Like Dubnyk, Rask is enjoying an NHL career that spans five hundred games, and is playing out a comfortable eight-year, US$56 million contract with the Boston Bruins. Today, Pogge's whereabouts elicits a nod from Rask, the way you greet news of an old classmate whose name you remember but whom you were never particularly close to.

"I shook his hand after the games," Rask said. "But I never talked with him."

"It was tougher than I thought."

Inevitably, Jeff Glass's World Juniors—his dream season—had concluded. So, too, had his teenage years. Glass wasn't a nineteen-year-old stopping pucks from sixteen- and seventeen-year-olds anymore. Now he was a pro, and at twenty years old, the Ottawa Senators third-rounder was back to being the youngest player at camp again.

"It was a Canadian market, I was coming off of winning the gold at the World Juniors, and I followed it up by being named Goalie of the Year in the CHL. I thought I'd had a pretty good year," Glass said. "I came into camp with high expectations, and I started the year in the East Coast League. I went down there right off the bat, and I was going to have to work from the bottom right on up. Nothing was given to me—I had to earn it."

Knowing now how Glass would have to scratch and claw for the next fourteen years to stay in the game, starting at the very bottom was simply a sign of what was to come. The problem was, like Pogge, Glass didn't know back then what he knows now.

"I don't think I accepted it well," he admitted. "Twenty-year-old Jeff Glass thought he was going to play for the Ottawa Senators. Walk right in. I figured, any time in the American League would just get me ready for the NHL. The East Coast League? That wasn't even on my radar.

"Looking back, a more mature Jeff Glass would have seen the opportunity I had in front of me and probably capitalized a little better than I did."

Glass had watched as so many of his Team Canada teammates became NHL regulars that fall, the straw he had drawn must have seemed particularly unfortunate. Over the years, the 2005 alums were named NHL All-Stars, hoisted Stanley Cups, and won the league's major awards. As the 2019–20 NHL season began, at least three—Brent Seabrook, Patrice Bergeron, and Dion Phaneuf—had played more than a thousand NHL games, while another seven players off that '05 Team Canada were well into the nine hundreds.

None of those players began their careers in the ECHL, as Glass did. Nor did they spend the next three seasons in the AHL.

"It was tough, but it kept me hungry. It's kept the engine going," said Glass. When we spoke, he was thirty-three years old, playing for head coach Dallas Eakins in San Diego in the AHL. "I've always had to kind of take a different path than everyone else. Every year, whether it was the year I spent in the East Coast League, or the three and a half years I spent in Binghamton, or going to Russia. Always seeing my colleagues, my friends, and former teammates in the NHL kept me hungry. And it still does.

"I love seeing those guys there, seeing how much success they've had. Some of them are going to be Hall of Famers, and other guys are still just scratching away. It keeps me loving the game, and wanting more."

The timing for Glass and the Senators just never seemed quite right. Brian Elliott, a ninth-round draft pick, leapfrogged Glass in the Sens organization, while Ray Emery was already in place when Glass arrived.

"There just wasn't room for Jeff Glass," he admitted, using the third person. "A more mature goalie would have handled that a little better, and maybe made room for himself one way or another. But I seemed to get frustrated, and couldn't quite crack it. Looking back, I don't know if it was an opportunity wasted. It was a tough situation for a young goalie, and time for the two sides to part ways.

"It was time for us to move on."

When the gold medal game began in 2006, Pogge had not faced more than 24 shots in a single game in the entire tournament. On average, he had seen just 18 pucks per game. The Russians were very confident in their ability to overwhelm Pogge, noting that he had not yet seen an attack like the one they would bring. They saw Canada's weak underbelly in the untested goaler.

"We can compete with them physically, but at the technical level we will beat them," said defenceman Andrey Zubarev, whose NHL career would play out five seasons later in the form of four games with the Atlanta Thrashers. "Historically, the Soviet type of hockey is more skillful. This game is no exception."

So much for Russian history. The next day, Canada would walk through the Russians 5–0. Pogge, who would play every minute of the tournament for Canada, turned aside 15 shots in period one alone and posted his third shutout of the tournament.

"I'll always remember it. The group of guys we had, closing out that final game in GM Place. It was surreal," Pogge said. "You know, there's always pressure. You're Team Canada—you're supposed to be the best. You're playing at home in Canada, and that year we didn't have all the studs, even though we did have Johnny Toews. I think any team with Johnny Toews on it is a good team, but we kind of had a group of misfits compared to the year before, which was the Dream Team."

As it turned out, Pogge was the Dream Goalie. It was only going to be a matter of time before he graduated from Christmastime on TSN to Saturday nights on *Hockey Night in Canada*. Or so thought the fans of the blue Maple Leaf. Toronto even cleared the tracks for Pogge that June when they traded Rask to the Bruins for goaltender Andrew Raycroft. It was a huge trade at the time, and even today it is fair to depict that deal as one that changed the course of two franchises.

"Raycroft was twenty-six at the time," Ferguson said. "We thought he would be an appropriate number one . . . that he could bridge a gap to Pogge. We gave him a three-year contract and hoped he'd be followed by Pogge. That was our projection."

It was a fair conclusion, and one that was summarily adopted by the collective hockey world, too. Pogge had been deemed the superior prospect, and Raycroft would step into a goaltending void in Toronto to carry the team through to Pogge's inevitable coronation. But when you were wearing Pogge's skates, that wasn't at all how things appeared.

"That story haunts me," he admitted. "I was a third-round pick [ninetieth overall in '04], one pick after Jeff Glass, actually. Tuukka was a first-round draft pick [in '05]. He was traded for Andrew Raycroft, and I think that's where everyone gets confused. The Leafs put their faith in Andrew Raycroft, and not me. It's been the storyline for a long time that they put their confidence in me [ahead of Rask]. No—they put their confidence in Andrew Raycroft. That's who they traded the first-round draft pick for."

Despite Ferguson's succession theory, Pogge had a point. At the time of the deal, Raycroft was just entering his prime as a goalie.

"He was a Calder Trophy winner. I think that's your guy," Pogge said. "That's how I looked at it. If I was their guy I would have had a spot on the roster in training camp."

And so began the process that regularly confuses fan bases across the NHL: drafting and development. Had the Leafs drafted the right goalie in Pogge but messed up his development? Or did they simply identify the best eighteen-year-old goalie, whose career peaked the next season, and whose game never developed?

After turning pro that fall, Pogge posted average numbers for a first-year AHL goalie: a 3.03 GAA with an .896 saves percentage. By his third season, he was still playing for the Toronto Marlies, and his saves percentage was .895. Zero progress. He became that goalie who goes up and down like a yo-yo, immediately reassigned for salary cap purposes after every call-up.

Pogge got his first NHL start on December 22, 2008, in Atlanta, stopped 19 of 21 shots for the win, then travelled with the Leafs to Washington before being sent down. He got another start on January 27 in Minnesota, stopped 15 of 21 and lost, and went back down. Pogge got into seven NHL games that season. He never posted another W, and never played another NHL game after that 2008–09 season.

Having dreamed of being an NHL goalie since he was a kid, Pogge—like Glass—discovered the hard way that the process was nothing like he had envisioned.

"Fly in the night before, have a pregame skate, and you're starting a game," he said. "I don't think I was put in the best position to succeed, but I was in a position. I had a chance."

Ferguson, who readily admits today that the Leafs made a regrettable deal when they shipped Rask out, posed the same questions over what failed Pogge. Was it the Leafs' role as developers? Or did the player's skills simply stop improving when he reached his twenties? Was that magical fortnight in Vancouver simply the peak of this player's athletic career?

"He relied too much on just being big, and could not improve his footwork or the technical aspects in his game. So many of the things that projected him to be a probable starter, or at least a backup, never improved," Ferguson said with the cold, clear assessment of a professional evaluator. "But also, there was a level of professional pressure to deal with, and I'm not sure that as an organization we did a very good job of shielding him from it. The [Rask] trade didn't help. Maybe if we retain Rask, it's a better competition as both guys work their way along.

"As an organization we might have been more marketing conscious than we should have been. I remember the first training camp that Carlo Colaiacovo was at, he was already on billboards inside our retail store. We had a larger than life poster of Justin Pogge—an action photo from his World Juniors in Team Canada equipment—at least fifteen feet tall on the outside of the ACC."

Eventually, when Ferguson was succeeded by Brian Burke as GM in Toronto, Pogge was dealt to Anaheim for picks. There, he backed up a few games but never played an NHL minute. He was loaned out from AHL Portland to Charlotte and then dealt to Carolina. It was a four-team season.

"It can get tough," Pogge said. "Living, playing in the minors can get taxing, with all the politics involved. 'Who's going where? And why isn't this guy getting his chance?' I had seven years of it, and I didn't want to go to the Coast [East Coast Hockey League], or some semiprofessional league."

Pogge lasted two more AHL seasons—a decent year in Charlotte and a not-so-great year in Portland, Maine—then cashed his chips in after the 2011–12 season.

Six pro seasons and seven pro teams since his World Juniors apex, Pogge was off to try his hand in Europe.

After eleven pro seasons—four in North America and seven abroad—Glass was still without an NHL game on his resume. He was, however, well stocked in accrued hockey knowledge. Today Glass speaks "emergency Russian" and survived his playing time in Siberia, where it once snowed for forty-five consecutive days.

Still, much like Pogge, Glass is an eternally positive person, and he appreciates what his extensive hockey travels have brought him, even if by 2017 it still had not included an NHL paycheck.

"Life experience," he declared. "I became a much better goalie over there, and learned a lot about myself. I'll never be one of those guys who bashes the KHL for the way they go about things. I'd be quite the opposite."

But in a conversation late in the 2015–16 season, while Glass was playing in Minsk, Belarus, his agent asked him if he still harboured any NHL dreams.

"I couldn't honestly say, 'No,'" Glass said. "He said, 'If you ever do want to do it, this is about it.' I was looking at opportunities to sign longer contracts overseas, and that would be it. It would mean never coming back again. I'd be too old, and that ship would have sailed."

A few months later, Glass was back in North America, standing between the pipes of Pogge's old team, the Toronto Marlies. Later that season, he was dealt to Chicago to play on the Blackhawks' farm team in Rockford, Illinois. Eventually, starter Corey Crawford got hurt, and the thirty-two-year-old backup was checking into an Edmonton hotel late at night after climbing off the team charter from Vancouver.

The goalie coach caught Jeff Glass just before the elevator doors closed. He had a message from head coach Joel Quenneville.

"Hey, you're starting tomorrow. You wanna skate in the morning?" the coach asked.

"Yeah, I do."

"I wish I was my thirty-three-year-old self when I was twenty," Justin Pogge said with a laugh, a twist on the old lament, "Too soon old, too late smart."

Pogge is content with where the game of hockey has taken him, even if he hasn't stopped a shot from his old teammate Johnny Toews in well over a decade. He is still playing, still earning, and seeing the world—all at the same time. Truly, it beats having a real job.

"I can make money at this, and in Europe, it's a lot easier to keep it in your bank account," said Pogge, whose professional hockey journey has wound through Italy, Slovakia, and a couple of stints in Sweden. "There is a lot less taxes, or teams are paying them. It's a good life, and you can really make it. You have six months where you don't have to pay rent. The lifestyle in Europe is great. Less games, you have a car [paid for by the team], my wife loves it here, my son was born here. The health care is great. It just seems like a logical choice once you kind of get pushed out of North America.

"I'll go until the game tells me I can't go. Body is good, and I feel like I'm playing better than I ever have. And I have the brain behind the body now."

That same brain won't let Pogge forget about the original plan, however. About the goals set by that Penticton kid twenty years ago, fulfilled by seven NHL games—one NHL win—but never fully satiated.

"I don't think that dream will ever die. To put on an NHL jersey again would be an amazing experience," he said. "I work as hard as I can during the season to have good enough stats that maybe someone will notice.

"Life's good here, but I'll never stop chasing that dream of playing in the NHL."

In the meantime, you'll find Pogge each Christmas—now with his son, Nash, in his arms—watching the red maple leaf. Sure, it's not the blue Maple Leaf, but it is the only maple leaf that ever loved Justin Pogge back.

"I'll always be so proud when I get to tell my son those stories, and he can see the tournament. See how big of a deal it is," he said.

When does Pogge buy Nash his first set of goalie pads?

"We're starting him off with a right-hand stick," he said. "If he wants to play, he'll be a defenceman. Like Erik Karlsson."

"Don't call, but find a way to get up here. I'm playing tomorrow."

Allie Glass got the text after 2:00 a.m. in Calgary. She was up, feeding two-month-old daughter Lucy.

"Just get yourself ready," she texted back. "I'll take care of everything."

Later that morning, December 29, 2017, her husband walked out of the sub-Artic Edmonton weather and into Rogers Place for a morning skate. Not to back up. For the first time since he was drafted back in June of 2004, Jeff Glass was slated to start that night against Connor McDavid and the Oilers.

A year before, during a call-up by the Blackhawks that never resulted in a minute of NHL ice time, goalie Scott Darling had talked with Glass about that moment they drop the puck in your first NHL game. "You become an NHLer. No one can ever take that away from you," he said. The hallowed NHL Guide and Record Book would reflect that fact forevermore—even if it was just for one night.

"I thought, 'Just drop that first puck,'" Glass said. "That means I become an NHL goalie."

When Glass arrived at the state-of-the-art Rogers Place, met there by his goalie coach with the Blackhawks—1988 World Juniors hero Jimmy Waite—he walked through the visitors' dressing room door, down the corridor with the stick racks on his left, past the coach's office, and toward the medical facilities straight ahead. When he made the left turn into the Blackhawks locker room, what do you think was showing on the big screen TV?

The outdoor game at the 2018 World Juniors in Buffalo, between Canada and the U.S.A.

"We were all watching the World Juniors," Glass said. "And then I got to play."

That evening, with Allie, Lucy, Glen, and Jane in the crowd, Glass would open the game by thwarting McDavid on a semi-breakaway. Then he bested Leon Draisaitl, who was in alone. He stopped 30 of 31 Oilers shots through two periods, accepted a welcoming tap on the pads from an uber-aware McDavid, and was only beaten by a deflected puck and second rebound chance that forced overtime. There, Patrick Kane's deadly dangle gave Glass the precious W that had evaded him for so long.

Glass made 42 saves and was, of course, named the game's First Star.

"Give him credit. He's waited his whole life for this," said then-Oilers head coach Todd McLellan. "He had a hell of a game."

Dressing across the visitors' room from Glass was Brent Seabrook, a defenceman off that 2005 World Juniors team who was playing career NHL game number 960.

"I was looking across the room at him, and it didn't seem like he was nervous," Seabrook said at the time. "He's thirty-two. I guess he's played a lot of hockey."

You think?

"We all had the dream of going to the NHL and playing long careers," Seabrook said. "It's just impressive determination by him to stick with it, then come tonight and play the way he did. A thirty-two-year-old rookie? First game in the NHL? We were all trying to play as hard as we could for him."

After the game, Glass could barely get through his media responsibilities fast enough, with his parents, wife, and daughter waiting for him near the bus. (Imagine, a guy who has had the football pulled away from him as many times as Glass has, and he names his daughter Lucy.)

"You know, so many people had supported me and helped me to get to that point in my career, I feel like I owed it to them," he said. "To sit back and say, thank you. I was pretty proud of that moment."

A couple of years after his NHL debut, Glass was back in North America and toiling on Anaheim's farm team. There are a couple of twenty-six-year-old kids he's battling for AHL ice time, but if they're smart, they'll be sponges around Glass. He, like Pogge, could be a tenured professor in the School of Hard Knocks.

"I'm proud of the way I did it. It wasn't conventional, that's for sure," Glass said. "Looking back, I made a lot of friendships, and I think I earned the respect of a lot of guys. I'm most proud of that. The way the guys played for me, not just in that game but over my career. I've always prided myself on being a pro."

As of the spring of 2019, Pogge had seven NHL appearances, and Glass had fifteen. Between them, they have four wins. That would be a good ten days' work for Rask, who best puts into words how a World

Juniors star can become a world traveller, his pads slung over one shoulder, an equipment bag hanging over the other.

"You know, you get drafted when you're eighteen, and the scouts see you as you are," Rask said. "They are projecting how you are going to be in five years, and sometimes those projections don't add up. You don't become the player they thought you would become, and you don't fit into the organization anymore.

"Next thing you know, you're out of time and you're playing in Europe."

It's always going to be a journey, but what we never know is where that journey will lead. For some, the World Juniors is a stepping stone; for others, it's the peak. But for all of them, it's a memory that never gets old.

CHAPTER 10

Products of Pressure

"I think that a lot of guys on that bench were hoping that their name wasn't called."

—CONNOR McDAVID

The people who have been where Maxime Comtois was asked to go, they know how lonely a place it can be. How much courage it takes to hop over those boards and be the lone player on whose shoulders an entire tournament rides. They've taken those penalty shots, or shootout attempts, and they've both succeeded and failed.

You may think you know what it's like to step into that moment. But you don't. They know—the Jordan Eberles, the Jonathan Toews, the Jarome Iginlas, the Max Comtoises—what Connor McDavid knows: "It's a brave thing to go out there and take that shot."

It was January of 2019 in Vancouver, a quarterfinal game against the Finns, where Comtois's moment arrived. After opening with a 14–1 win over Denmark, then beating the Swiss 3–2 and the Czechs 5–1, Canada's offence had run dry. They scored just once in their final round-robin game against Russia, a 2–1 loss.

Suddenly, Canada found itself in a sudden-death game against Finland, which had beaten them soundly in pretournament action. Canada's powerplay was on an 0-for-8 run, and after a lucky Finnish goal tied the game with forty-seven seconds left in regulation, Canada was headed to a 1–1 overtime nail-biter. It was one of those "next goal wins" scenarios that tends to fade into history when Canada wins and moves on, but that gets etched into our history books in perpetuity when things go the other way.

Early in overtime, Canadian defenceman Evan Bouchard was hauled down on a breakaway, and a rare overtime penalty shot was awarded. A full house of more than seventeen thousand people buzzed as Team Canada head coach Tim Hunter and his assistants mulled over who would take the shot, while TSN analyst Ray Ferraro listed off three possibilities. Finally, Maxime Comtois emerged from the bench and skated toward the Canadian blue-line.

"And he's going to go with the captain, Comtois," said Ferraro on the TSN broadcast. As Comtois circled near the Canadian blue-line and began to pick up some speed, Ferraro exclaimed, "What a pressure-packed moment!"

Unbeknownst to Canadians, Comtois was nursing a shoulder injury late in the tournament. But he'd been healthy enough to play in the quarterfinal, and he'd performed pretty well. Hunter would later say that he and his coaching staff had decided that, should such a do-or-die situation ever arise in the tournament, Comtois would be the chosen shooter.

On any Canadian roster in any WJC, there are three or four players for whom you could make a case to be the shooter in a situation like that—in 2019, Owen Tippett was an excellent option, as was Morgan Frost or Cody Glass. On the ice, that means that every Canadian roster has enough snipers to present a threat in any situation. Off the ice, it allows for plenty of second-guessing if things don't go as planned.

Hunter no doubt knew about Comtois's injured shoulder—the Ducks prospect would go to Anaheim for treatment after the tournament. But Hunter stayed on plan and sent his captain out to shoot.

"There are so many things going through your mind. It's overtime, and you have a chance to put it away," said Comtois, who was finishing his final season of junior with the Drummondville Voltigeurs in 2018–19. "We practiced shootouts before the tournament. It was a pressure moment, and I was still confident. I was hoping my name would be called. I'm one of those players who wants the puck on his stick to win a game.

"I was confident, going in to do my move, trying to get us the win."

Gord Miller took over from Ferraro as Comtois collected the puck at centre ice. "In comes Max Comtois, with a chance to send Canada to the semis! Comtois holds. And shoots! And Luukkonen makes the save . . ."

Comtois snapped a shot low-blocker, but Finnish goalie Ukko-Pekka Luukkonen—whose lightning-fast legs made him the media All-Star goalie at the 2019 WJC—made the toe save to keep his team alive.

That moment would be a life-changer for Comtois. He just didn't know it at the time.

Moments later, Canada would have another chance to win the game in overtime. Trailing defenceman Noah Dobson stared at an empty net as he began his downswing on what was a fairly routine one-timer for a player of his skill. Dobson turned his hips and stroked through the puck in perfect form. However, his stick betrayed him, snapping at the exact moment he needed it the most.

Down came the Finns to the Canadian end, where Toni Utunen—who had not scored a goal all season long—fired a hopeful wrist shot. The puck hit the shaft of Cody Glass's stick and went top shelf past Canadian goalie Mike DiPietro, who had been brilliant.

Canada's tournament was over.

It was the first time Team Canada had ever failed to medal in a tournament held on home soil, and Comtois was not only the captain of the sunken ship, but also the guy who missed the penalty shot that would have put Canada into the semifinals.

Sour Canadians, some of whom had already criticized Comtois for a couple of perceived dives during the tournament, took to the Twitter, piling onto the nineteen-year-old hockey player with negative posts. Comtois faced the media in Vancouver postgame, as any stand-up captain would and should. But after that evening at Rogers Arena, he went quiet. The next the country heard of him was in a press release issued by his agent, Allain Roy.

"Maxime Comtois is the ultimate example of a Hockey Canada athlete who has grown through the ranks to become a selfless leader. No one is prouder to wear the maple leaf on his chest and C on his jersey," the statement began.

"It is shameful and incomprehensible that a few cowards who can hide behind social media could make such vicious attacks on these young men's character after they have battled their hearts out for their country.

"It was Maxime's idea to use this as a learning moment for all the youth of Canada, that cyberbullying is a real problem, and like all bullies, we all need to stand up to them and call them out for what they are."

Comtois shut down comments on his Instagram account and stayed off Twitter. Two months after the tournament ended, though, he seemed back in a healthy place.

"After what happened, I was trying to get out of [Vancouver] as quickly as possible," Comtois said. "When you look back now though, it's a bad experience but you've got to learn from those things. Yes, it is a high-pressure tournament—especially for Canada—but I wouldn't change anything. I would jump into that tournament again tomorrow, if I could do it again."

As a player who has spent a lifetime "playing up"—and who has still been the best player on his team most years, regardless of how much younger he was than everyone else—Connor McDavid is one of the few who is able to speak to the yoke of responsibility that burdened Comtois that January evening in Vancouver.

"I bet when that penalty shot was called there were some guys trying to make themselves pretty small. Which is normal," McDavid said. "That's not a fun place to be in, and even though there were for sure a couple of guys that were ready to be the big hero, I bet you there were a lot of guys who didn't want it."

As a generational player, McDavid clearly knows success. But failure is to success what engagement is to marriage. Every groom must know both, and McDavid experienced his own such moment in Malmö.

"It was a game against the Czechs," he recalled. "We were in the round-robin, and we were not supposed to be in that shootout with the Czechs at all, so the pressure was on. [As the thirteenth forward under Brent Sutter] I was not playing at all.

"It came down to our turn to shoot, and someone needed to score to keep it going. I shot, and I hadn't touched a puck—touched the ice—in an hour and a half. I missed, obviously, and we lost the game to the Czechs.

His move?

"A little backhand-forehand thing that didn't have a chance."

It's a lot of pressure for a sixteen-year-old to be under, as McDavid found in that tournament.

"It's a lot of pressure for anyone," he corrected. "Everyone in that tournament is young."

Andrew Cogliano, who won back-to-back gold medals in 2006 and 2007, got a Master Class in shootout pressure watching Jonathan Toews work his magic in that legendary semifinal game against the United States, a tilt that stands as one of most dramatic games in the history of the Program of Excellence.

As he had been in the eye of the hurricane, the irritation in Cogliano's voice was palpable when he spoke to what Comtois went through.

"After a guy misses, you get the people on social media, and you get all the wannabes who really don't know anything and never really played," Cogliano said. "McDavid's right: Half of that bench doesn't want to take that shot.

"I didn't like what happened there. I commend the kid for wanting to shoot. For wanting to be out there in that situation. Because I'm telling you, in Vancouver in that moment, I guarantee you there were plenty of guys who didn't want to take that shot."

Cogliano knows of what he speaks. In 2007, Canada and the U.S. remained tied after regulation and overtime, pushing the two teams to a shootout. American goalie Jeff Frazee stopped Steve Downie and Bryan Little on Canada's first two shots, while Peter Mueller slipped one past Carey Price on the Americans' second attempt.

Jonathan Toews had to score to keep things going on the third attempt, and he zipped a low wrist shot past Frazee. After another save by Price, the teams entered the second stage of the shootout, which, under quirky IIHF rules, allowed Canadian head coach Craig Hartsburg to go back to whichever player he wanted, as often as he wanted. Hartsburg wasn't just smart enough to go back to Toews when the rules allowed it. He would go back twice.

"There were nerves," said Cogliano, who sat on that bench at the Ejendals Arena in Leksand, Sweden, that day as the shootout unfolded. "Not that guys didn't want to shoot, but it was a pretty big stage. With Toews, guys just felt like he just looked fairly confident. Like he really knew what he was doing on breakaways. When he scored on the first one, it looked like he knew what he was doing. Hartsy's mind was made up. [Toews] was one of our most skilled guys, and obviously it was the right play. Talk about one of the most impressive things you've ever seen: A guy goes on three shootout attempts, makes three different moves, and scores on all three of them. In that situation!"

In round four of the shootout, Hartsburg went back to Little, who scored. Toews went top cheese in round five. And in the sixth round, Hartsburg—similar to the way Dave King had looked down his bench in search of a face-off winner and found Troy Murray some twenty-six years before—looked down his bench, casting about for a shootout hero.

"You have half the bench that's second-guessing themselves, thinking, 'Man, I don't want to be the guy who screws this up.' Especially with how the Americans were scoring," Cogliano said. "I remember looking back and making eye contact with Hartsburg, and I remember him calling me."

Cogliano was resigned to the moment. Fate had put him under

the brightest of lights, so there was nothing to do but get out there and give it the best he had.

It was one of those, "All right. Here it goes," moments. Cogliano hopped over the boards with a gold medal on the line.

"I think I shot low-glove, and the chances of scoring low-glove on a shot are so few and far between, you'll rarely see it—even in the NHL," Cogliano said. "This one, it turned out as good as it possibly could. Jack Johnson came down the next shot [for the Americans] and buried one."

In the next round—the seventh of the shootout—Toews deked Frazee, authoring his third goal of the shootout. Now, it was Price's turn to feel the spotlight.

The Americans sent out Mueller to take their attempt. Mueller played his junior hockey with the Everett Silvertips, a WHL divisional foe of Price's Tri-City Americans, and Price had a book on Mueller, whether or not the American knew it. Even though Mueller had equaled Toews with a pair of successful attempts on Price, the future Habs franchise goalie banked on Mueller reverting to his go-to move.

"I was just sitting on that five-hole shot," Price said, "because he had beaten me with it when he was playing for Everett. He didn't use it the first two times, but I was sitting on it."

Price read the play perfectly, and when Mueller snapped the shot, Price shut the door. The Canadians piled off the bench and mobbed Price, celebrating as though they'd already won the gold medal.

Canada would go on to defeat Russia in the gold medal game, without the aid of a shootout. It became one of those tournaments remembered more for its fabulous semifinal than for what happened in the gold medal game, much like the 2009 tournament in Ottawa, remembered for Jordan Eberle's semifinal heroics.

In a shootout as elongated as the one in that 2007 semifinal game, it's pretty much impossible to find a goal to hang the loss on. Comtois's penalty shot was the opposite—had he scored, it would have been game over in Canada's favour. There have been lots of shootouts at the World Juniors, but almost zero penalty shots of as much consequence as the one Comtois took. What occurred was a delayed scapegoating, one that had to wait until a few more things went wrong and Canada lost the game in overtime. Had they won, you'd be reading about something else on this particular page.

Goaltenders are used to that type of selective scrutiny. They can let in a stinky goal in the third period, but if their team manages to win anyhow, social media and radio talk shows move to a different element of the game. If their team loses, though, it becomes all about the bad goal they allowed.

Roberto Luongo lost his gold medal game in overtime in Winnipeg in 1999, his second World Juniors tournament. He saw the social media backlash aimed at Comtois and, looking at it not just as a goalie but also as a parent, thought it was a bit much.

"Sometimes, everybody has got to just take a little bit of a step back," Luongo said. "It's hockey, it's a tournament that we all want to win, but we've just got to realize that these are kids, and they're trying the best they can to represent their country well. I'm sure that the kid was more heartbroken than anyone else was. So take a little bit of a step back and realize that we're playing a game. Do whatever it takes to win, sure. But there are other teams playing as well. Sometimes you're not going to come out on the winning side of it. That's the reality of sports."

After backing up Mathieu Garon in the Canadian debacle that was 1998 in Helsinki, Canada rode Luongo to a gold medal game in 1999 against Russia. The Russian team didn't have a lot of big names on its roster, but it was everything the Canadians could handle.

"I'd played well the whole tournament, feeling good about where my game was at. Feeling some nerves, but excited to play," said Luongo. He carried his team into overtime in the finals, where Artem Chubarov set up in the slot and took a pass from Maxim Afinogenov before blistering a tournament-winning snapshot past Luongo.

"It was kind of a one-timer, and I think he kind of missed his shot," Luongo recalled. "He didn't really get all of it, so when I went to make the glove save, his body motion—where he was shooting the puck—it ended up not going exactly where he was planning to shoot it. It ended up being a little lower, and it went off the bottom of my glove and into the net."

The lasting camera angle that branded itself on Paul Romanuk's memory was from the net cam, as the reality of the loss dawned on Luongo. It was over, and Canada had lost. He wouldn't get a second chance on that Chubarov shot or another shot at a World Juniors gold medal that Christmas.

It was a lot to process in those devastating few seconds.

"I was crying," Luongo said. "Everyone was crying after the game. Just because it was such a grind, the whole tournament, and we were right there—overtime in the final. It was heartbreaking.

"You know, when you're a kid you don't really know how to respond to those kind of moments. The emotions got the best of me at that point, and I started crying."

But then the people of Winnipeg did something Luongo will never forget. After Chubarov's goal, as the Canadian players picked themselves up from the ice, so, too, did the fans rise from their seats. They applauded players from both teams for having played one of the most entertaining gold medal games in World Juniors history, and they made it a point to serenade Luongo, the poor Montreal kid who had lain on his back in tears, as the celebrating Russians dog-piled in the Canadian zone.

"The crowd. That was something that really stuck with me," Luongo said. "They were chanting my name after the game, and it really made me feel better. When it was said and done, after we'd lost that game, the crowd was still with us. I'll never forget that."

It didn't take long for Winnipeggers, as Luongo said, to "take a step back."

"It's a good point by [Luongo]," Comtois said. "There's a lot of pressure on the program, and we're only nineteen years old. We've got our whole careers in front of us—if you lose, this is not the end for you."

Sure, fans who pay their money earn the right to cheer or boo. But how far does that privilege extend? And does social media give those who haven't invested a penny in the process the right to dismantle a person online just because a penalty shot didn't go their way?

"We work so hard, and this is our dream," Comtois said. "Every player in Canada dreams to play for that gold medal at the World Juniors during Christmastime. People who don't play hockey or aren't involved in sport, they don't know all the sacrifices that players make to be there, to keep progressing and trying to be better. We're going to do anything to win, but they forget: Other countries are good, too."

It's so simple to boil a game down to a single play, as if the other fifty-nine minutes and fifty-nine seconds had nothing to do with the result. Like those who say that Steve Smith cost the Edmonton Oilers their five-in-a-row Stanley Cup streak when he banked that shot into Edmonton's goal off goalie Grant Fuhr's ankle back in 1986. That thinking couldn't be further from reality, something many fans don't realize, but it's a fact that every person inside the game is acutely aware of.

"We didn't lose because I missed my penalty shot," Comtois said. "We were in the lead late in the third, and we gave up a goal with forty-seven seconds left to go in regulation. We had our chance in overtime: a three-on-two where we had a broken stick. It went down the other way, the guy's shot went off a stick and in.

"People forget, [a penalty shot] is a one-on-one. The best player in the NHL, he goes 35, 30 percent in shootouts. I was confident with my move, confident in my ability to score, and it didn't work out. At the end of the day, I would take that shot any time."

The one question mark that arose in the aftermath of the Canadian loss—and it is a fair question to ask—pertained to Comtois's shoulder injury. It is one thing to allow your captain to play hurt—that's just part of hockey lore. But should he have been the one selected to take that shot with the game on the line?

Chris Pronger, for one, didn't think so.

"Here's a question: Why is Comtois getting ripped?" Pronger asked in the days after the social media story had gone public. "I would ask, 'Why is the coach putting him out there?' Do you know how many goal scorers were sitting on that bench who would have loved to take that shot?

"And then we find out he had a shoulder [injury]? What are you thinking? [Tim Hunter] had to know he had an injury. Why aren't you using Cody Glass? Or Owen Tippett? Or one of those kids who relish that situation? That's why they're there."

The sheer audacity of people piling on a kid whom they were cheering wildly for only moments before is not lost on Pronger, a notoriously straight shooter.

"Do you think he didn't want to score? I mean, how stupid is that? Why are you treating a kid like that?" he asked. "The kid tried his best, and he didn't score. And, by the way, now we go back and look at the goalie, and it turns out the kid's pretty good."

Comtois admits that his shoulder was "pretty bad. I injured myself in the third game of the round-robin, but I wanted to play. I was captain of the team, and I didn't want to watch my team from upstairs. I wanted an impact on the game."

Hunter knew the risks, and he didn't put more pressure on Comtois's shoulders than he thought his captain would be able to handle. Luukkonen made the save, but the result shouldn't change everything that preceded the moment, should it?

It comes back to the amount of pressure we apply to teenagers who give themselves to the World Juniors tournament. The coast-to-coast television. The sold-out NHL arenas. The "gold or bust" expectation that Hockey Canada itself once thought was too much, but today is resigned to.

Jarome Iginla saw all of the Comtois fallout, and it got him to thinking. Iginla has three kids now, all of whom play high-level hockey. One day, he might be sitting in the stands watching a son or daughter in that situation, which is an entirely different scenario than living through it himself.

"When you're part of sports you realize, penalty shots and the percentages and all of that—they can go either way," Iginla said. "But I do like the pressure. I think it helps the kids, no matter whether they get to experience the good or the bad side of it, the winning and losing. I think it's great for their growth."

The way minor hockey has gone—the increased number of games each year, the heightened expectations of parents who invest thousands of dollars into a single season, the agents and junior teams that scout fourteen-year-old Bantams—the pressure kind of helps, when you think about it.

It was the mandate of the Program of Excellence to introduce elite Canadian players to a higher level of hockey—and pressure—as young teenagers, all so that they would be more ready to excel in U-20 and Olympic play.

Iginla can still remember that day back in St. Albert, Alberta, when the kitchen phone rang and he was invited to a tryout camp for Team Pacific as a fifteen-year-old. He went to Calgary, made the team, and journeyed to Amos, Quebec, for his first taste of what was to come.

"It felt like a really big deal," he said, sporting his ever-present smile. "They gave you jackets!"

Of course, it's not about the jackets. It's about experiencing competition.

A kid taking a face-off in overtime of an all-Ontario tournament as a fourteen-year-old wants to win that game as much as Crosby wants to win Game 7 of the Stanley Cup Final. The will, the wanting—it's no different for any elite player. The only thing that changes is the size and importance of the trophy.

"It's not like you just get thrown into the Olympics," Iginla explained. "I look back at each of those steps I got to take and I feel like it was part of a building process that helped me to get used to the pressure. To enjoy it.

"I really did enjoy playing in those situations, and playing in the Olympics in Vancouver. I know it went the right way, but we also lost in Torino. Part of sports is, it's more fun to play in games when there's more on the line. It does hurt, but you learn a lot when you don't win. No matter whether you get to go on further, just being part of the World Juniors is awesome for the kids that do it."

Iginla was Team Canada's star in his only World Juniors, held in Boston in 1996. He carried Canada through that tournament, the same way he carried the Calgary Flames to Game 7 of the 2004 Stanley Cup Final. But right before those World Juniors had opened, the Dallas Stars—which had drafted Iginla eleventh overall in 1995—traded him to Calgary for longtime Flames fan favourite Joe Nieuwendyk. It was a lot for the young player to digest: cast off by the team that drafted him, replacing a pillar from the Flames' 1989 Stanley Cup champion team; a kid from an Edmonton suburb, now suddenly a Calgary Flame.

Then, as if an eighteen-year-old could handle anything more, the tournament began. Iginla would score 5 goals and tally 12 points in six games. Physically, he was a beast. Mentally, you couldn't have put more on an eighteen-year-old's plate than the Hockey Gods had doled out to Iginla that Christmas.

Oh, and by the way, Canada was riding a three-year gold medal skein. Losing in Boston? It was not an option.

"You were expected to win a gold medal, that was the pressure, and they talked about it," he said. "Hockey Canada didn't shield you from that pressure. They'd hang faxes [from fans back home] around the dressing room every day, people cheering you on, and it was cool. But at the same time, the expectation wasn't, 'Boy, I hope we can have a good showing. Maybe get a silver.' It was always all about gold, and it was the same way on every single Canada team I ever played on, from Under-18, to World Juniors, to the Olympics. It was always the same mentality.

"You embraced it. It was always gold or bust."

On what was literally Iginla's final international shift for Canada, it all came together. Everything that Murray Costello and Dennis McDonald had imagined transpired in overtime of that gold medal game in Vancouver. Crosby yelled, "Iggy!", accepted the pass from Iginla, and deposited the golden goal behind American Ryan Miller.

That play, and those players, weren't just players for the Program of Excellence. They were products of it and the pressure therein.

"Each time you go through those situations, sometimes you get too excited, sometimes you get nervous," Iginla said. "I remember being in Vancouver [in 2010], and you knew before you went out for that game it was going to be either an amazing story or a story that stings for a long time. It's exciting, and you go out there and try to stay in the moment.

"But every one of them, from Team Pacific, to U-18, to World Juniors, they helped me in my career. Every time you have success it builds a little more grit, and every time you don't you try to learn from it. 'Okay, what can I change?'"

No matter whom you talk to, the one consistent thread among Team Canada alumni is a unilateral agreement that the pressure we put on our Canadian kids is not too much. You simply cannot find a successful hockey person who would shield our elite teenagers from that spotlight.

"Yes, there is pressure. But I don't know any nineteen-year-old hockey player who wouldn't trade places with them," said Marc Habscheid, who both played and coached Team Canada at the WJC. "It's high-stakes hockey. You'll be remembered for scoring a winning goal, or maybe you'll be remembered for something negative you did. It's unfortunate, but that's hockey. That's life, and you can't insulate them forever. I'm okay with it."

The unintended consequence, of course, has become the lack of interest and effort in the bronze medal game. Whether it was the lost bronze medal game at the 1988 Olympics or the bronze medal game at the 2014 World Juniors that McDavid played in, Canadian teams have been accused of bringing less than their best once the gold medal is no longer within reach.

"For us, the tournament was over," said McDavid, whose Canadians lost 2–1 to Russia in the bronze medal game in 2014. "It's gold or bust for Canada at the World Juniors. It's gold or bust for Canada at any tournament we play in. That's the way it should be."

With that pressure, of course, come the rewards for those who become heroes. Like John Slaney, who scored the gold medal winner in '91. Or Jordan Eberle, who played in two WJCs and was a household name in Canada by the time he was done.

"My family, we based our Christmas holidays around World Juniors. I remember Grand Forks, seeing Sid. I remember Pierre McGuire's calls, the Double Dion. I grew up with all that," said Eberle, a Regina kid who has always had a knack for the hardest thing to do in the sport—scoring goals. "It was always a goal of mine to make that team, and I was lucky enough to play twice—and both in Canada. Super, super, special for me."

Eberle's moment came in Ottawa in 2009, when he scored with 5.4 seconds remaining in a semifinal game to get Canada into overtime against Russia. The goal, even though it did not actually win anything for Canada, has somehow gained a spot in our national hockey consciousness among the biggest ever scored.

We'll forget about Comtois's penalty shot attempt over time, but can you not still picture Eberle in front of the Russian goalie, going forehand-backhand and lifting the puck into the net as he fell to one knee?

What other Canadian goals have stayed in your memory like that? Paul Henderson in '72, of course. Mario Lemieux at the 1987 Canada Cup? Crosby's Golden Goal in 2010?

That Eberle's goal, scored in a semifinal game, has found that kind of company in the Canadian hockey consciousness speaks to what the World Juniors have become in this country.

"If it wasn't such a big goal I wouldn't remember it. But people have asked me so many times about it, I've replayed it so many times," said Eberle when asked to walk through the moment. "There were a couple of icings, which kind of gave us a chance. They tried to rim it out, and we made a good play to keep it in along the wall. I think it was [Cody] Hodgson who threw it back in along the wall. [John] Tavares kind of threw it at the net, and [Dmitri] Kulikov misplayed it.

"I always say, I was in the right spot at the right time, and I was able to finish it off."

With that, Jordan Eberle's Max Comtois Moment became something he'll talk about until he's a little old man, a clip that will play the rest of Eberle's life whenever his name comes up.

If you or I scored a goal like that in beer league we'd replay it to our buddies with infinitely greater detail, aggrandizing our own personal role in the play. If somehow we could make the goal sound more important, we would, like any good fish story.

The experience of playing in the World Juniors today is most often one of the premier memories in a hockey career. Seldom does a player like McDavid admit, "I didn't enjoy my first World Juniors experience," or say, as John Slaney did of the debacle in Fussen, "I really don't want to talk about it."

And even when things don't go as planned, there's something to be learned. "I've learned in my career, sometimes the heartbreak and the hardship is what makes you stronger and better as a person," Luongo said.

There are no promises when you put on that Team Canada jersey, there is no template to follow—even though, over the decades, Hockey Canada likes to think that it has put together a pretty good roadmap to success.

For Comtois, the memories of the ignorant trolls will fade away. You can tell when you speak to him that those objects in his rearview mirror are already smaller than they appear. Like Eberle, Iginla, or Luongo, he'll cherish being part of that special club—the Canadian hockey kid who grew up dreaming of pulling on a Team Canada jersey at Christmastime.

"I will remember every moment of my two experiences there," Comtois said. "The first one, as a kid who nobody really saw playing a solid tournament, and helping to develop my game and put a name on me. To Vancouver, and being the only returning player and the captain.

"It's a dream playing for Hockey Canada, and being the captain means the world for me—that the staff, the whole organization of Team Canada believed in my ability to lead this team to a gold medal.

"I didn't do it, but it was an awesome experience. Just like any player, it's probably the best moment in their life."

CHAPTER 11

Shouldering the Captaincy

It turns out that being the captain of a Canadian World Junior team comes with some drama. Who knew? Well, guys like Troy Murray or Max Comtois, they knew.

Step right up, Barrett Hayton, who in January 2020 became the latest in a long line of Team Canada captains to learn that a tiny piece of fabric in the shape of a "C" can weigh far more than you would ever dream. As we have learned over the years, the making of a good captain requires the same elements that form diamonds: heat, plenty of pressure, and time.

Of course, before Hayton could submit himself to the experience, the National Hockey League team that drafted him—the Arizona Coyotes—had to agree to release him.

"He made our roster out of camp," said Coyotes general manager John Chayka. "But the way our team started—we were first in the division—we didn't have a lot of injuries and we had a lot of veteran guys who were playing pretty well. As a result, his ability to get ice time and make an impact just wasn't there, through no fault of his own. Our team was healthy, we were playing pretty well, and we traded for Taylor Hall [a few days after releasing Hayton]. It became a much easier decision to allow him to go have that great experience."

As a returning veteran from the 2019 team in Vancouver and Victoria, Hayton knew exactly what he was stepping into. He flew up to Canada in December, then "kinda just met the team, had a shortened camp, and flew over to Europe."

Hayton couldn't wait for a second chance at the World Juniors. He had watched from the bench the year before when Finland's Toni Utunen took a shot that ricocheted off of the shaft of Cody Glass's stick and flew over goalie Mike DiPietro's shoulder. It was the final blow in a series of events that forged perhaps the luckiest victory in a hockey game that this reporter has ever witnessed.

"From the bench it felt like slow motion," is how Hayton recalls it. "You saw the guy wind up to shoot, it hit something, and it ends up going top shelf. You couldn't believe it on the bench. It didn't feel like it was real. One of the strangest feelings I've ever had in my life. Pure heartbreak. The most heartbreaking, sunken feeling you can have." This was the canvas, as a returning vet, upon which Hayton hoped to paint a vastly different piece of art. Then, on Christmas Day, the stakes were raised even higher.

"We had a great group of leaders. Nobody knew how it was going to play out, because there was a ton of options," he said. "I came in the room, we had a little team meeting, and they announced the leadership group. Nothing too crazy." But the crazy was yet to come for Barrett Hayton, who was named Team Canada's captain that day.

"It's a unique circumstance, [the World Juniors] being such a short-term event," said Hayton the following summer as he rode out the COVID-19 stoppage as a full-time boarder at teammate Jason Demers's Arizona home. "When you're the captain of a team for a full season, or an extended period of time, you can lay it out a lot differently. But at the World Juniors, it's about just trying to get the guys bought in, get everyone on the same page. You have to identify those fine details that really make a difference in such a short tournament."

One thing we've learned over the years is that being a captain of a hockey team has taken on an entirely new meaning since the old days when Mark Messier—not the Edmonton Oilers captain at the time but surely a leader—would call a postpractice meeting at a local tavern, attendance at which was considered compulsory. It wasn't about the beer. It was about the team being a team away from the arena, and not just inside the confines of the rink.

For a junior team that comes together for roughly a month, the parameters are completely different. Team Canada isn't about the slow build, or even forging relationships that last for a lifetime (even though that happens every year). It's about getting the program to a competitive level quickly, and then recognizing the moments as they come when a veteran can save his younger teammates a session or two at the School of Hard Knocks.

"There are other responsibilities—a lot of media requirements, etc.—but really the biggest thing is just being a guy [players can] go to," Hayton said. "There are so many leaders on that team, who wear letters with their club teams, it's not much rah-rah. It's structured [around] guys you can go to for advice, often guys who had played the year before.

"It's really about experience. All the guys, they're such good players. But you really can't relate that tournament to anything else you've ever experienced, with the stage it's on. So it becomes about getting guys bought in in the short term, and being a go-to guy in games when someone has to step up and push the pace. Be someone who guys can look to for energy, and try to match it. There are a lot of different factors in such a short tournament."

Hayton learned pretty quickly that being a leader is not about what you say. It's about what you do.

"Absolutely—at that level it's all off of your actions," he said. "You can say whatever you like. At the end of the day it comes down to what you do and what you show."

Ironically, at the 2020 tournament in the Moravian-Silesian region of the Czech Republic—played in the cities of Ostrava and Trinec—what Hayton showed early on was not what would be defined as leadership. He found himself in the middle of an international incident just two games into the tournament. Of all people to forget to take their helmet off for the postgame anthem, as a sign of respect for the nation whose anthem was being played, the last person that you would expect to make that mistake would be Canada's captain.

"At that point we had played three pretournament games," began Hayton. "We were three-for-three, and had [beaten] a really good Finland team in the final pretournament game. Coming off the first game against the U.S., a strong game for us [6–4 win], we had a lot of confidence. And I think, rightfully so."

The Russians were up next, and it was not only in the 2020 tournament that each side saw the other as an early-tournament measuring stick. The result of the game wasn't the be all and end all—the Canadians just wanted to know that their best game at that point was close to or better than Russia's best game.

Everyone was going to raise their level from there, and both sides knew it. But an early Canada-Russia game is still a Canada-Russia game, so when Hayton's squad fell behind 3–0 in the first period, it rattled the Canadians.

"One fluky goal, and they made some great plays and put a couple of other ones in. It caught us off guard. Kinda shocked us," said Hayton, whose charges would give up another three unanswered in the second period, eventually losing 6–0. "They dominated us that game. It was just something where you were trying to comprehend what happened. Comprehend how to go forward. What adjustments we needed to make.

"In a short tournament, you build confidence but it can get struck down just like that. You've kind of got to look at your identity and—not necessarily reevaluate—but look deeper into what's going on. There was a lot going on there."

For a captain whose ship was suddenly listing, Hayton's head was spinning. Losing was one thing, but *six–nothing*? Where do you start rebuilding confidence after a butt-kicking like that one? It would be hard to identify which element was most lacking in Canada's game when in reality every part of it was weak that day.

What does a captain say after a game like this? Or, do you say nothing and wait until practice the next day, or the moments before the next game, two days later against Germany? Meanwhile, the teams lined up on their respective blue-lines as the Russian anthem played.

"I was just zoned out. Or, zoned into what had happened in the game," Hayton said. "As a player, my strongest asset is my hockey IQ. Just being one of those players who remembers every play. I break things down a lot. That's just how I am as an athlete—I just kind of remember all of that stuff. I like to review it and break it down and learn from it. At that point I was just trying to go through the whole game and figure things out.

"We turned around when the anthem played, and I was just staring straight ahead. I started going through the handshake line, and the first couple of guys shook my hand. After that, there was a group of guys who didn't. I was confused at that point. I realized it when I was coming off the ice. I knew I was in trouble."

As the anthem ended, Grigori Denisenko, the Russian captain, approached the referee to complain. He and several other Russian players refused to shake Hayton's hand postgame. Hayton knew he'd made a mistake, and that his inattentiveness might also be construed as disrespect for the Russians and their anthem.

"How that would come across, regardless of anything else that happened? I was concerned," he said. "I felt bad. Just being such a gesture that can come across as a meaningful thing—I immediately tried to explain it to our staff."

Before Hayton had even taken his equipment off and hit the shower, social media had taken the ball and folks were running with it online. It's a "cancel culture" that Max Comtois had experienced twelve months earlier when he missed an overtime penalty shot in a game that would see Canada eliminated. Now Canadians were calling for Hayton to be stripped of his captaincy, or kicked off the team.

And not just the usual keyboard warriors. Even ex–NHL player Devin Setoguchi called it on Twitter "one of the most embarrassing acts of character I have ever seen in hockey. Needs to issue a statement of apology now . . . or cut him mid tournament."

Hayton knew he was in trouble, but with no cell phones or access to social media, thankfully he was spared the public flogging. He'd made a mistake, and he was now focused on getting past it and not allowing it to weigh on a Team Canada that already had a few things to deal with.

"The biggest thing was trying to apologize to the Russians. Their team, and their country as a whole. I wasn't too worried about the social media stuff. I was trying to make things right with [the Russians]," he said. "Sure, with social media there are a lot of opinions, a lot going on. But being able to issue a formal apology to the Russians, kind of making things right on that platform, was the most important thing in my mind."

And so, through Hockey Canada, Hayton apologized: *"I'm sorry for leaving my helmet on for the Russian anthem following today's game, and I apologize to the Russian team and its fans. As a leader on this team, I was trying to process the game and evaluate how we can regroup. I was lost in the moment. The Russians played a great game tonight, and my actions were not intended to be disrespectful. My mistake should not distract from their win. I owe it to my team and all Canadians to be better."*

Kids, eh?

It's a good thing they can forget about a problem as fast as they can wade into one, and that's what Hayton and the Canadians did, bouncing back with a dominant win over Germany. Canada would finish the preliminary round in first place in Group B (after Russian losses to the United States and the hometown Czechs), and roll past Slovakia in a 6–1 quarterfinal win.

Next up was Finland in the semifinal, and the returnees had learned the painful lesson of allowing the pesky Finns to hang around. The Canadians came out flying: Connor McMichael scored just 1:48 into the game; Alexis Lafrenière made it 2–0 just seventy-seven seconds later. Then, just fifty seconds after that, Jamie Drysdale made it 3–0. The players went to the dressing room with a 4–0 lead, and it was as if the new Finnish team was paying the tab that the 2019 Finns had stuck Canada with.

The game was completely under control, with Canada ahead 5–0 in the third period, when Hayton busted down the left side in pursuit of a puck in the Finland zone, battling Finnish defenceman and Ottawa draft Lassi Thomson for possession. It was an innocuous play at a harmless point in the game. The two engaged and slid together into the end boards.

Hayton rose up from the carnage, the weight of his left arm being borne by his right hand as he skated to the Canadian bench. It was the classic sign of a shoulder separation, less than twenty-four hours from puck drop in the gold medal game.

"It was a routine battle. I kind of caught a nick in the ice and we both went down, with some pretty good speed. Kind of flew into the boards at an awkward angle, with my arm extended, and his body came in, too, to add to the force into the boards."

His shoulder was in bad shape—indeed, separated—and Hayton didn't even have an off day to rehab it. He woke up on the morning of the gold medal game knowing he might not be able to play.

"If I'm being honest, there was more than a chance. It was pretty much the bottom line. That was the thought process all along," he said. Doctors set him up with some anti-inflammatories, and Hayton went to bed hoping for a miracle.

Ironically, the year before, his captain, Max Comtois, had endured the same thing, though his shoulder injury had come during the preliminary round. Remember this quote from Comtois? "I injured myself in the third game of the round-robin, but I wanted to play. I was captain of the team, and I didn't want to watch my team from upstairs. I wanted an impact on the game."

That's how Hayton, or how any Canadian hockey player who reaches this level, is raised to think. It's easy to talk about how others played through the pain, however. It's something else to do it yourself.

"Going to bed that night, not really sleeping much, and the

worst part was waking up in the morning. Trying to sit up and get out of bed," said Hayton, who could feel all the muscles around the injured area engaging in strange ways, either injured themselves or compensating for the compromised shoulder muscles. "I give all the credit to our training staff, the work that they did to get it to the point where I could go out there and have a positive impact on the game."

Chayka had been receiving almost hourly updates, and decided to put his trust in the Team Canada doctors. "It wasn't a good injury, but it wasn't an injury that was going to get worse—by too much," said Chayka, who had "a lot of conversations. I talked with Barrett, his parents, the whole deal."

This is where, like the NHL's concussion protocol, the decision has to be taken out of the player's hands. History tells us they will endure any amount of pain, and reel off any litany of untruths, to gain medical clearance.

"All the doctors knew I would have played that game with a broken leg, if I could have," Hayton said. "With any hockey player at that point, it's about the doctor's [determination] on whether it is safe to play. Whether you can protect yourself. At those high stakes—the gold medal game at the World Juniors—you have to pass tests, have mobility and strength. I can honestly say this for all hockey players: There is no injury that's going to hold you back from attempting to play in that game. Whether the doctors clear you or not."

Chayka knew he had to give his young prospect the chance to make something special out of this. "To win, you're going to go through adversity. We felt like it would be taking away from the spirit of the player, the spirit of the competition, to take it out of his hands—as long as it's the right decision."

The year before, Hayton had watched Comtois play through his shoulder injury. He saw his captain fight through the pain and remain a positive force inside that Team Canada dressing room. Now it was his turn, and he didn't have to look very far to see a teammate doing the same thing.

In the preliminary round, in that 6–0 loss to Russia, the expected number one overall NHL draft pick, Alexis Lafrenière, injured a knee. At first it appeared as if he had torn everything there is to tear in a hockey player's knee. When the swelling subsided, however, there was Lafrenière, dressing for the quarterfinal game.

"That's the Hockey Canada slogan, the Canadian way," Hayton said. "Alexi, he had a tremendous tournament. Fortunately, he could get back and play at somewhere close to 100 percent. He's fortunate it wasn't worse, but yes, it's kind of a staple of Canadian hockey."

Canada got its rematch with Russia in that 2020 Gold Medal Final and got out of the first period tied 0–0. Much better. Then they answered a Russian goal to tie the game 1–1 in the middle period, before Russia scored again to hold a 2–1 lead after two periods. A tight, tough game between two equal teams was unfolding at the Ostravar Arena, and if the World Juniors tournament has taught us anything, it was almost a certainty that some drama lay ahead in the final twenty minutes.

As for Hayton's ability to contribute, he had twenty minutes left in his junior career to get something done. "The whole buildup was trying to go out in warm-ups and trying to shoot, and really easing into it. I think I had a couple of shots earlier in the game that I didn't really lean into."

After the teams traded goals, Hayton would have his "Comtois moment," as head coach Dale Hunter sent him over the boards for a crucial powerplay with just less than nine minutes to play in a game they trailed 3–2. For Hunter to put Hayton out in a shooting position—a left-hand shot on the right half wall—was akin to head coach Tim Hunter choosing the banged-up Comtois for the overtime penalty shot in 2019.

But this decision had a better outcome for Canada.

"We had two flank options," Hayton explained. "I could come downhill and make a play, or shoot. We had [Calen] Addison at the top, who is so good at moving the puck and kind of feeding the guys' lanes. Lafrenière dragged his guy down, made him move his stick. It went up to the top, a little pump fake by Addison, and he kicked it over to me.

"The majority of the time I pull it and shoot, but as the tournament went on, teams were prescouting that. So I pushed it out a little bit and let it go far side. Tried to get it up high over his shoulder," Hayton said. "I put everything I had into it. Just let it go, and see how it works out."

The puck sailed perfectly into the far, top corner behind Russian goalie Amir Miftakhov. It was pure fiction that a guy whose shoulder was in as bad a shape as Hayton's could fire a puck like that, and storybook stuff that it would find twine to knot the game at 3–3. "Honestly, one of the best feelings—probably THE best feeling—of my life. You just kind of go numb," he said.

The seldom-used Akil Thomas, who only played 5:23 in the gold medal game, chipped home the game winner with 3:58 to play. Lafrenière would have a two-assist game on his injured knee, and Hayton's goal produced another moment of Canadian World Junior lore that will live on in highlight form for decades.

This was the Program of Excellence the way it was drawn up so many years ago by those who pioneered the concept.

"The Hockey Canada slogan, the Canadian way: Having guys step up," Hayton said. "Akil Thomas is a star on his junior team and a tremendous player—so skilled, so versatile—and being able to play in special roles. That's the great thing about the World Juniors. Guys come in as stars—like Akil, who had 100 points in the OHL the year before—and he just takes that one opportunity and he makes the most of it to win us that gold medal.

"Alexi, he had a tremendous tournament. Fortunately he could get back and play. He's fortunate it wasn't worse. Ya, it's kind of a staple in Canadian hockey."

Chayka looks back on the decision he made to allow Hayton to play with a measure of relief that nothing bad happened, but also with the knowledge that sometimes you have to take a chance to reap life's rewards. There are no hero stories written on the trainer's table or in the press box, right?

"If we really wanted to pull the plug, we probably could have," said Chayka. "But, as much as people talk about the winning experience, nobody talks about when Barrett forgot to take off his helmet. Then he gets injured. The reality is, everyone thinks it's a straight line to the top—but it involves a lot of ups and downs, and adversity. As much as I would have loved for him to go there, stay healthy, lead the tournament in scoring, and win a gold medal, I really think he got the best possible experience, dealing with the ups, downs, and adversity along the way. You don't wish those instances on anybody, but in life they happen. The way he dealt with it will help him in the future with that journey to the top."

After the game, TSN's Tessa Bonhomme asked Hayton on live network television how his shoulder felt. With his gold medal around his neck, and a mile-wide smile on his lips, he replied: "Like a million bucks!"

He laughs about the quote, months later. "I wasn't lyin' at that point. I couldn't feel a thing," said Hayton, whose final game as a U-20 is one he will never forget.

"It is, honestly, fitting to say it is a roller coaster," he said. "My entire World Junior experience is a Cinderella story, going from worst-case scenario in Vancouver—the first time ever that Canada hadn't medaled on home soil—to everything that happened in the Czech Republic. Losing to Russia, and all of that—it kind of came full circle.

"Everyone can relate to a story like that. It can be really motivational for all walks of life. I am incredibly fortunate to have had the experiences that I have had. And ending it the way we did? It's a perfect way to go out."

EPILOGUE

Brent Sutter has been the face for the relentless, responsible, elite brand of Canadian hockey that has dominated the World Juniors tournament. But after losing in the semifinal in 2014, a decisive 5–1 spanking courtesy of Finland, Sutter had some news for Canadians.

"This is not just our game anymore," he told the media in his postgame address. "These countries take pride in playing the game at a high level and developing great prospects and great players. Us being Canadian, we expect and want to win all the time. But there is a lot more to it than that."

And so the circle of hockey life continues. After starting near the bottom back in the 1980s, Canada built a program that dominated the U-20 level for the better part of twenty-five years. Today, Canada is chasing once again. The team's results over the past ten years show a far more even playing field. Since 2010, Finland and the U.S.A.

each have three gold medals to Canada's two; Russia has eight medals overall and the U.S.A. seven, to Canada's six.

"We want to think it is Canada's game, and rightly so," Sutter says today. "Yet, you're not just going to win it because you're Canada, you know? That's where things have changed a lot over the years. Countries have caught up to Canada."

There is some irony that the Program of Excellence was initially conceived because a handful of Canadian hockey men could no longer stand to see something less than our best travel overseas to become fodder for the Soviets at the World Juniors every year. Forty years later, the Canadian program has soared to such heights that now it has become the benchmark, and others have hunted us down the way we did the USSR, back in the day.

In 2019, as I was filing the final words for this book, Canada had lost to the eventual gold medal winners from Finland at the World Juniors, while the Finnish women's team had upset Canada in a semifinal at the Women's World Championships. The players expected to claim the top two spots at the 2019 NHL Entry Draft were an American (Jack Hughes) and a Finn (Kaapo Kakko)—which is exactly what happened.

The U.S.A. Hockey National Team Development Program is primarily responsible for the fact that Canadians no longer occupy more than half of NHL roster spots, and it was born—to a large extent—as a response to Canadian dominance at the amateur levels.

Finland, a country of 5.5 million people—or roughly one-seventh the size of Canada—has built a system with full-time head coaches at the U-20, U-18, and U-16 levels, as well as a full-time general manager who oversees the program. Their junior hockey system is unlike ours, where players spend the season with CHL teams that are run like businesses, loaning their players out at Christmastime. Finland runs a national junior program all season long, and they're free to borrow U-20 players from the Finnish professional league when the national team attends tournaments.

And many of those young players are competing professionally. The advent of the KHL has created professional roster spots at home for younger Finnish players, who are steeled by playing against men, unlike their Canadian counterparts who compete against kids their own age. And Finland's location allows for more international competition over the course of the season, which leaves them more prepared to play as a team when Christmas arrives.

"I think most of the countries, now, realize just how much work you have to do," said Kimmo Oikarinen, the GM of the Finnish program. "And at the same time, in Europe this [World Juniors] tournament is getting bigger, and bigger, and bigger. That puts pressure on the [federations] to work more and more. It's a big tournament now in Europe, when it used to be only like that in Canada."

Look at how the Canadian program improved after TSN arrived on the scene, and Canadians discovered the gem that this tournament is. Now, as Europeans discover what we already know, so, too, do they expect their teams to be competitive when they tune in to watch. It's no different in Sweden than in Canada: If the home team wins, the TV ratings are higher. And if the TV ratings are higher, everyone makes more money.

So, perhaps Canada's greatest success in the hockey world isn't all those gold medals. Maybe it is creating a bar that the rest of the world has risen to meet.

"Nations like Switzerland, Denmark, Germany," said Swiss coach Christian Wohlwend, "are doing a fantastic job, with this [small] amount of players. Finland and Sweden have three times the players than us, and Canada maybe one hundred times. But we have this know-how now in the other countries.

"But Canada? Best hockey nation, for sure. By far the most amount of players, on this talent level. They will win, in the future, a lot of medals. Don't worry about Canada."

Perhaps the most tangible contribution the World Juniors tournament has made to international hockey was revealed as the 2019 tournament wrapped up in Vancouver. There, at his tournament-closing news conference, International Ice Hockey Federation President René Fasel made a surprising announcement.

"In Beijing, at the 2022 Olympics, if [the NHL] is there, we will ask the organizers to play on the small ice. And in Finland in 2022, we will play on small ice at our World Championship," Fasel said. "The future is having the best players of the world playing on the small ice. Why should we not be playing on the small ice?"

Fasel has been president of the IIHF since 1994, and despite his Swiss roots, he has watched how different the game is when it's played on the smaller, North American surface (200 x 85 feet, or roughly 26 x 61 metres) compared to the larger European sheet (roughly 200 x 100 feet, or exactly 30 x 60 metres). As the speed of players has increased and the skills of the youngest players has risen to places we never imagined, Fasel has realized what most hockey people would argue: Smaller confines call for quicker decisions. That means more mistakes, which leads to more chances on goal, and in general, that lends itself to a faster and more exciting brand of hockey.

"It is a different game, especially for the juniors, and the women's game also," Fasel said of the smaller ice. "It [produces] another game. For the hockey fan—a different game than we played . . . even five years ago. The young players here, [Patrik] Laine and [Connor] McDavid, and all of these ninteen- and twenty-year-olds [at the WJC]. . . . Can you imagine that these guys would ever be able to play the game at this [speed]? I don't think so."

The large European surface has given license to European coaches to devise defensive systems that rob the game of creativity, and defenders in Europe allow opponents to hang on to the puck on the perimeter, as it is so much farther from the goal. The art of goaltending has progressed faster in Europe than in North America, with training methods and a developmental system that have seen five of the past seven Vezina winners hailing from Europe, as well as two of three candidates in 2018–19.

Teemu Selänne, the great Finnish Flash who had 10 points in seven games at the 1989 WJC, once described what the biggest difference was between the big and small surfaces. He gave the example of being on the half-wall just above the hashmarks, and attacking the opponents' net.

"When I beat the defenceman coming off the wall in the NHL, I take one, maybe two strides and I am at the goal in prime shooting position," Selänne said. "In Europe, if I beat the defenceman I still need three or four strides to get to the same position. But by then, the other defenceman has come over to cut me off. So now, I have to beat two players to get the same shot."

But seriously. Playing on small ice at the World Championships in Finland?

Could you imagine if the biggest tournament of the season—say, a Canada Cup or a World Cup of Hockey—was held in Toronto, and organizers informed Canadians they would use a different-sized ice surface from the one we have used for more than a hundred years?

It will take a while for larger rinks to be phased out across Europe, or for new ones to be built that can transition to both sizes. But perhaps if the U-20 game can sell Fasel on the concept, it can convince hockey fans in Europe that there is one more element of Canadian hockey that is worth emulating.

"You can say that Canadians care more about the World Juniors than any other country, and that's true at the basic fan level," said former Canadian coach Perry Pearn. "But with all the ability to see games, read about it on your phone . . . the young players in Sweden, Finland, and Russia, they know what's going on. And they all have dreams, too, whether it's to play on their national team, or play in the NHL."

Even with their growing success, most Europeans still defer to Canada when it comes to the organizational success we've made of the World Juniors tournament. The tournament has become an annual benchmark for progress across the pond, as European tournament organizers consider how close they can come in terms of profits and attendance to the events held in Canada.

"What is important to know," said Luc Tardif, Sr., the head of the French Ice Hockey Federation, "is that if all those countries accept to come to Canada every second year, that means they like to play in front of that attendance, the professional [element] of the organization.

"But there is still a big gap to go. The [2020 tournament] is in the Czech Republic, but everyone will be happy to come back to Edmonton in two years."

Whatever the future holds, one thing is for sure—they'll keep coming back. Players, teams, fans, they all keep coming back. To the home of the World Junior Hockey Championship.

ACKNOWLEDGEMENTS

Murray Costello had no idea how many phone calls and emails he was in for when he agreed to tell me the story of that meeting at the Skyline Hotel in Ottawa and the birth of the Program of Excellence. Nor did Bruce Newton, when I stumbled across his name as a longstanding Hockey Canada employee. Troy Murray, Paul Romanuk, Dennis McDonald, Jim Hughson, Bob McKenzie, Brian Williams, and Michael Farber were all vital sources of information—voices who were there, who took me back to those crucial moments that made this book possible. Thank you to you all.

Of all the former and current players in this book I've had a working relationship with, Brendan Shanahan took time away from one of the highest offices in Canadian hockey to take me back to Piestany, as did Chris Joseph, only weeks after he'd suffered the unimaginable loss of his son Jaxon in the Humboldt bus crash. Justin Pogge and Jeff

Glass entertained me on the concept of having starred in a World Juniors yet never having significant NHL careers, and generously talked me through their unique and compelling travels.

When researching, Wikipedia, HockeyDB, and QuantHockey made this book possible, as did Gare Joyce's fine compendium for Hockey Canada, *Thirty Years of Going for Gold at the World Juniors*.

And many thanks to Canadian hockey fans, without whom I would have to find a real job.